BUILD A BETTER ATHLETE

What's Wrong With American Sports and How to Fix It

Dr. Michael Yessis

equilibrium
books
A Division of Wish Publishing

LCCN: 2005936065

Editorial assistance provided by Cristina Gowrylow and Dorothy Chambers
Indexed by Adrian Mather
Cover designed by Phil Velikan

Cover photography used by arrangment with www. photos.com. Interior photography provided by Dr. Michael Yessis and by arrangement with www.photos.com

Printed in the United States of America
10 9 8 7 6 5 4 3 2 1

Published in the United States by
Equilibrium Books, A Division of Wish Publishing
P.O. Box 10337
Terre Haute, Indiana 47801, USA
www.wishpublishing.com

Distributed in the United States by
Cardinal Publishers Group
Indianapolis, Indiana 46218

Table of Contents

Acknowledgments

I am deeply indebted to many people who have helped make this book possible. Without their persistence and sometimes perseverance this book would not have many of its unique and informative features. The order in which the names appear is not related to the importance of the work and the assistance that they have provided. More specifically I would like to thank:

- Brad Albert for his great work in helping capture video clips of selected athletes and importing them into the computer. In addition he helped generate the pictures needed to show the specific actions or sequence of actions. He is presently Director of Tennis at the Dana Hills Tennis Club.

- Marissa Yessis my wonderful daughter for her great work in importing video film into the computer and selecting the necessary frames for the sequence pictures and exercises. In addition, she served as a model for some of the skills and exercises illustrated.

- Bryan Canfield who served as a model for some of the baseball throwing pictures.

- Glen Reyes who served as a model for some of the running, cutting and baseball throwing pictures.

- John Campbell who served as one of the models for sprint technique and various exercises for explosive power.

- Joey Campbell who served as the model for pictures of a young runner.

- Dianne Denechochea, professional beach volleyball player, who has trained with me for several years and who served as a model for some pictures.

- Tammy Leibl, a professional beach volleyball player who plays with Dianne.

- Hector Mateus, who served a model for some of the soccer kicking pictures

- Jerry Singleton, a model for the football throwing pictures.

- The many athletes with whom I have worked. Some of them also served as models for the various exercise pictures and for the skill cinematograms. They have already been acknowledged in other books and are thus not individually thanked at this time. I apologize for any that I may have missed. Without these many athletes who practiced many of the exercises and training regimens, this book would not have been possible.

- Mary Lou Isbell for her great assistance in keyboarding and helping with the many revisions.

- Edie Yessis, my lovely wife, for her comments, suggestions and support during the writing of this book.

- Holly Kondras, editor and publisher, who provided valuable help in shaping the final product and especially the cover.

Introduction

This book contains a great deal of information, more than you typically find in a sports book. The information presented is based on the latest we know in theory and from practical experience. All of the methods and recommendations have been tested and proven to be effective.

Some of the information may be hard to grasp at first reading, especially if your background in this area is not strong. However, I have tried to present the material in a straight forward manner so that it can be understood by experts and novices alike. Thus, do not be discouraged when you come to a section that appears to be beyond your abilities. Reread the section or continue reading and then go back to it at a later date.

Much of the information is illustrated with sequence pictures taken from videotape. Especially informative are the cinematograms taken of athletes executing their respective skills. Thus, you are seeing "live" execution, not posed pictures as are typically shown in most sports books.

You will also see that the execution by the individuals is not perfect, that each has some very strong and weak points. This is typical of most athletes and is the reason there is always much room for improvement regardless of the level of performance.

Many of the strength exercises are not illustrated mainly because most of the exercises are fairly well-known. Adding all of the pictures and their descriptions would in essence be writing another book. However, if you need more information, see *Kinesiology of Exercise*, the most detailed book available on strength exercises.

As you read the material, make notes, comments and suggestions to yourself in the margins or in the blank space found at the end of each chapter. When you do this you will be actively engaging your brain as you read the material. You will be questioning and reacting to it. Through this process, the information will have a greater impact and you will develop a much better understanding of it.

Reading and comprehending the material is similar to learning a new skill. When you first played golf (or tennis, etc.), you probably whiffed the ball quite a few times or had some terrible hits. In time, with a sufficient number of repetitions you began to develop the skill and hit the ball well. The same process applies to reading and mastering the material here. It may take a few repetitions, but then it will come to you and remain with you, especially as you put it into practice.

When you apply this information you will see immediate results. You will not have to wait one, two or three years to become a better player or coach. The changes and improvements will be seen quite soon, within the time allotments needed for true changes to take place. For example, it takes six to eight weeks before there are true physiological strength changes.

This book is not a cookbook. It does not simply give you recipes to follow to automatically become a better athlete. The reason for this is simple. There is no one recipe that fits all athletes. All recipes (training programs) must be adjusted to the sport, age, sex, fitness level, skill mastery, nutrition availability and so on of each individual.

Presented instead are guidelines and information that you can incorporate into your work to develop and improve athletic performance. If you still have questions after reading the book, you are welcome to send them to the website, www.DrYessis.com. All of the most frequently asked questions will be answered on the website. Individual consultations will also be available.

In the next chapter you will learn about the present status of player development in the United States. My companion book, *Sports, Is it All B.S.?*, has much more detail dealing with this topic and presents many specific examples of commonly believed myths (B.S.) and myths in specific sports. Reading this companion book will give you additional background to better understand the need for the information presented in *Build a Better Athlete*.

Chapter 1
The Current Scene

For years coaches have believed that good athletes are born – are "naturals" – and that you cannot improve the techniques of running, hitting, kicking, throwing or other skills. The overwhelming belief is that you must already possess the technical skills and physical abilities to play the game; if not, you will not make the team. Coaches see their role as motivators and strategists to blend a team into a functional unit. They say they teach the basics of the game, but this means basic strategy, not skills. When skills are taught, the teaching is superficial and short-lived.

The general recommendation for improving player abilities is to play more and do drills: To become a better player you must devote more time to playing the game and practicing game skills. But is this the best way to become a better player? No, because you do not improve your technique and physical abilities when playing. Any improvement in technique is usually by chance, repeating the same skill performed well many times to develop a pattern of movement that can be repeated in basically the same manner.

For example, runners are told to run faster and longer, while kickers are told to kick more to improve distance and accuracy. Tennis players are advised to hit more balls and to participate in more competitions. Swimmers are told to increase distance, while throwers (javelin, shot-put, discus throw) are told to throw more and to weight train. In golf it is now common to see high-level players hitting up to 500 or more balls a day! Overlooked in this push for more playing and practice time is mastering and perfecting the specific sports skills.

When Do You Start?

Most parents start their youngsters in sports at about age 5. Many youngsters start earlier. After reading that Tiger Woods started playing golf at age 2, many parents follow his footsteps with their children. The practice of starting youngsters at very early ages stems from what was believed to be the way the Soviets and East Germans produced such outstanding athletes in the 1960s-80s. The media, in an effort to sensationalize, constantly repeated that the Russians and East Germans would literally take children out of their cribs and mold them into outstanding athletes. The media refused to look at what was done to train the athletes, when they truly started serious training and how the whole training system was set up.

If they had looked closely, they would have discovered that Soviet and East German athletes, especially those in team sports, did not begin to specialize until the ages of 13 or 14. Prior to that time, they were exposed to different sports in which they learned many skills. As these skills were mastered, coaches evaluated their performances and then recommended that certain athletes specialize in specific sports because they were more suited for them. The earliest an athlete started serious training was 5 to 6 years of age, and this was only in the sports of gymnastics, swimming, ballet and figure skating, which require years of serious work on technique and/or development of specific body functions.

Figure 1.1: Ballet

Do Genetics Make You Great?

Genetics are often touted as the reason for an athlete's success. It does play a significant role in some sports, but genetics account for only about 30 percent of your abilities, while environmental factors — your training and lifestyle — account for 70 percent of your success.

Figure 1.2: Playing ball

The role of genetics has been greatly overplayed by coaches as a way of explaining why some athletes are so much better than others. This is also how the concept of the "natural" athlete arose. But close examination of the natural athlete shows that he or she is capable of playing more than one sport and excelling at each. When these athletes undertake a new sport they master it quickly and can play on the same level as some of the best players in that sport.

Individuals become naturals because of their participation in sports activities in their youth. A youngster who participates in many different sports at an early age develops the basic neuromuscular pathways that are used in almost all sports. Thus, when they take up a new sport they already have the basic coordination and movements established. This makes it relatively simple to add the finer points of the new sports skills. Success is partially due to genetics, but mainly due to early training and participation in a multitude of sports.

Genetics are significant on the extremes of a normal distribution among the athletic population. A few athletes possess up to 95 percent white, explosive muscle fibers, while at the other extreme a few possess up to 95 percent red, slow-twitch muscle fibers. In between, most athletes have a more equal or somewhat skewed distribution of muscle fibers.

White muscle fibers play an important role in speed and explosive events. To be a world-class sprinter you must have a predominance of white fibers. An athlete who has a predominance of red fibers will never become a world champion in the sprints no matter how much or how hard he trains.

A predominance of red fibers can make you most successful in endurance events. Thus to be a world-class marathoner or ultra-distance runner, swimmer or cyclist you must have a predominance of red, slow-twitch fibers. An athlete with a predominance of white explosive fibers will never be able to run the distance at the speed exhibited by top long distance runners with a predominance of red fibers.

Since most athletes have a more equal combination of red and white fibers, they become successful in team sports. A high percentage of red or white fibers is a detriment to becoming successful in a team sport! For example, in basketball or volleyball, sports in which you must do a great deal of jumping and exhibit quick bursts of speed, you must have well-developed white fibers for the explosive actions and well-developed red fibers to last the entire game.

Even though you are born with a certain distribution of red and white fibers, it does not mean you will automatically be able to display the qualities which they help determine. You must still train to exhibit the actions for which these fibers are responsible.

Is There a Training System?

There is no basic system of training athletes in the United States, except playing in higher leagues. The only common factor is weight training for building strength and thus developing a better player physically. The lack of a system has spawned organizations to keep track of budding "stars." Records are kept on 10- to 11-year old players in different sports, especially in baseball and basketball, so that teams and sports companies have an inside track to signing them.

What is disheartening about this practice is that youngsters who show potential but do not yet possess the skill levels of star players are often disregarded. Yet these are often players who, with additional smart training, could equal and even surpass elite players! Understand that most youngsters who go through puberty early are typically the better players in the youth leagues. But those who mature late can easily catch up and in many cases surpass their peers in athletic abilities with the proper training.

Dropouts are very common in teenage years because of late maturation and lack of playing skills. For example, in baseball and softball, if you cannot hit, throw or field the ball well, you get little satisfaction from playing, even though your team may win every game. If you aspire to be an athlete you must get satisfaction and fun from playing because you can execute the skills that are involved.

In most youth leagues there are always a few fortunate youngsters who, through trial and error, early maturation, or exceptional physical attributes, become more successful in executing game skills and as a result become successful players. Other players on the team then serve to enhance the progress of a few. More effective would be a system by which the youngsters could first master the basic skills before they competed seriously in the sport.

Mere exposure to a skill — as often occurs in youth leagues and in physical education classes — does not produce true learning. For example, in a typical class or team of 20 to 30 youngsters with one instructor, the instructor may introduce the rudiments of a skill and the youngsters may practice it for five to 10 minutes. The next day instruction is given on another skill, with little time devoted to practice until the basic skills of the sport are covered in only one to two weeks, and then competition begins.

I feel confident if you look back to the earliest days when you participated in sports, you will not be able to recall teachers or coaches who worked on your technique on a daily basis, or who worked with you until you could execute a skill so well it became automatic, before you participated in league competition.

Even on the professional levels, there is no system of training to improve athletic performance. Minor leagues are set up for more playing with the hope that the better players will soon be identified — similar to the cream rising to the top in natural milk. The most prevalent method of training is strength training, but the types of programs used and the selection of exercises leave much to be desired. Very often the methods used at the professional level are the same as those used for the general population. This may be fine for general conditioning but not for specialized sports training.

Coaches' Qualifications

Figure 1.3: Coach with athletes

Most coaches lack knowledge in the area of sports skills. They do not have the background to understand what is involved in the execution of different skills nor the expertise to teach them. They may have a background in the sport, but it is usually in the area of strategy, not skill development. This is usually not the coaches' fault since universities rarely teach skill development to teachers or students in sports classes on all levels of education. Coaches and teachers are primarily concerned with practice, organization, motivational and tactical aspects of competition to prepare for game play.

Because coaches see their job mainly as putting a team together and preparing it for competition, recruiting plays an important role on the professional, university and even some high school levels. In most of the major universities, recruiting has a multimillion-dollar budget. Coaches look for the best players who already have the skills, just as they do on professional levels. Teams buy (recruit) an athlete to fill a gap they have on the team; they do not recruit an athlete who only has the potential to be great.

There are no major certification programs for coaches; those that do exist are very basic, and cover only the rudiments of the sport. There are no in-depth programs to develop knowledgeable and expert coaches who understand what is involved in sports skills and how athletes can truly improve their performance.

Because a coach may have a winning season does not mean he had the best training program. In reality, it usually means he had the best athletes to produce a winning team. In most cases the best coaches in the world would not be considered the best coaches if they did not also have the best athletes.

This trend may be changing in the near future as more parents learn what can be done to improve their youngster's performance. Parents are willing to invest money (sometimes considerable amounts) to improve their youngster's sports performance in the hopes that he or she will be able to get a college scholarship or become a professional athlete.

Finding a true expert may be difficult, but using some of the principles, guidelines and information presented in this book can go a long way to producing a better athlete and coach. Everyone can improve, including a professional athlete. I have yet to meet an athlete who could not be better!

For more information regarding the current scene and the misinformation and myths that have permeated sports in the United States, read *Sports: Is It All B.S.?* It is a great complement to this book and substantiates the need for better player development.

NOTES:

Chapter 2
The Road to Mastery

If you are a parent with a son or daughter involved in sports or an aspiring athlete or coach, you may be somewhat depressed after reading the first chapter. It does not present a very promising outlook, especially if you let nature take its course. But if you are serious about improving sports performance, you can help yourself or anyone you're working with to become much better than they are. Everyone can make tremendous progress. Most serious athletes can easily get college scholarships and some can make it to the pros.

Most important to realize is that everyone can improve greatly, much more so than if they only play the sport and do the usual weight training, stretching and/or use of steroids. Young athletes usually make great progress, but understand that much of it is due to maturation. This occurs naturally, not necessarily because of the coaching or teaching that is done.

Training plays a major role prior to puberty, especially in the area of skill development, in learning different exercises and training methods, and in becoming accustomed to exercises that will be done with greater intensity at a later age. Beware of coaches who tout themselves as sports specialists, especially in the areas of strength, speed and quickness, since the programs advocated are typically physical conditioning programs.

Figure 2.1: Swimming

For example, I have spoken to many athletes who, after working with the Yessis System of Improving Performance, have gone to professionally funded training camps to improve speed. For three weeks they were involved in heavy weight training and stretching. Drills and exercises for speed and quickness were done, but the players experienced little to no gains and felt the camps were of little value. Many of them became slower because of the training, especially the high-intensity weight training. Out-of-shape and novice athletes did, however, improve but not to a level that surpassed their best playing level.

To become a better athlete, you must work on two key areas: technique (how well you execute the skills involved in the sport) and development of the physical abilities (strength, speed, power, etc.) as they relate to the technique. Combining physical ability development with technique improvement is the ideal situation that results in the fastest and most productive improvement in sports performance.

The key is to develop your physical abilities in relation to the technique. Both are worked on independently but most often used together in very specific ways. The more effectively you execute the technique and the greater your physical abilities as they relate to your technique, the more effectively you can execute the skills in game competition. This is the key to a successful performance.

Development of technical and physical aspects of performance also play an important role in improving the mental and psychological attributes necessary for the best performances. For example, the more proficient you become in executing the skills involved in the sport, the greater will be your confidence level. You will feel secure knowing that not only will you be able to execute the skill when it is called for in a game situation, but you will be also able to execute it so well that you can repeat it every time. You can become the "go-to" player. Without this technical and physical base, psychological training will have little value in improving your performance.

Getting Started

The question you are probably now asking is what should you do and how should you get started? The answers depend upon your age, physical abilities, sex, sport, skill mastery, level of game play, etc. First you should determine when to start serious training. Understand that some sports require very young participation, especially if technique is crucial to success. This includes ballet, swimming, figure skating, gymnastics and to a certain extent, endurance events.

There are several factors involved here, but suffice to say that you must begin to specialize in these sports at an early age because it takes many years to master the technique and the physical and mental qualities that are needed to succeed. For example, in women's gymnastics and figure skating, world champions are usually in their teenage years. For men, it is usually in their twenties. Thus, knowing the number of years it takes to master the skills and abilities to participate on a world-class level dictates when you must get started.

Other sports, especially dual and team sports, require early participation in a multitude of sports with specialization occurring at a later age. For example, soccer, football, baseball, lacrosse and tennis require some early learning of the basic skills and rudimentary strategy. However, other sports should also be played throughout the year as there is great cross-over at this time. Doing this enables the young athlete to develop more of his physical skills, coordination and basics of strategy, which are similar in team sports in the early years.

All athletes will experience success on many different levels, but the long-term goals should be kept in mind at all times. More specifically, you must develop a multiyear program broken down into four phases: phase one, universality; phase two, specialization; phase three, competition; phase four, transition. The exact ages for each phase varies depending upon your sport. To achieve the most success in your sport, you must go through these four phases.

I. Universality (aka The All-Around Phase)

In the phase of universality, you become an all-around athlete and develop athleticism. You do many different types of training and play a variety of sports to learn different basic skills and coordination patterns. This phase is devoted to strengthening the body, especially the muscles, joints, ligaments and tendons as well as the functions of the body, such as the cardiovascular, respiratory and nervous systems. All of the body functions and systems are interrelated and do not work independently in the execution of sports skills.

For example, you need the nervous system to coordinate with the muscular system to stimulate the muscles to contract with the right amount of force, duration and timing. The nervous and muscular systems combined are known as the neuromuscular system, which is involved in all sports skills and is the basis for sports technique and body coordination. The more developed the neuromuscular system is, the easier it is to learn the basic skills of running, jumping, throwing, hitting, kicking, etc., and to do various exercises for strength, flexibility, agility, speed and technique. When well-developed, the neuromuscular system is also responsible for preventing injury.

Development of the cardiovascular system at an early age is extremely important for all athletes, not just for endurance athletes. When you play a sport, even though you may only use quick bursts of speed

Figure 2.2: Playing soccer

or power for short periods of time, you must still be able to recover as quickly as possible. This can only be achieved through the efficiency of the cardiovascular and respiratory systems. Thus the key in the early years is to develop all the prerequisites for participation on a higher level in a particular sport. This is also the way to maximize your genetic capabilities.

It is important to distinguish training versus playing. The key for young athletes is to stay away from serious training. At this stage, it is most important to gain exposure to sports, to learn the basic skills, and to develop the body. In this way you do not physically or psychologically overload the athlete. When you begin serious training, the physiological and psychological or mental aspects become very important.

Whenever I think about universality I recall a young Russian athlete I watched in an international volleyball match. Even though he was a junior he played with the national Ukrainian team because of his great skills. It was hard to identify his strongest abilities and American and foreign coaches were amazed at his great playing. He was a great spiker, setter, passer and receiver, and his movements on the court were excellent. This is an outstanding example of what can be gained through the development of different skills. In questioning him I found out that he was not only very adept at volleyball but also basketball and soccer. However, he wanted to specialize in volleyball.

When you think of universality, think of exposure to many different sports and skills to attain a broad all-around foundation. By doing this, the muscles, joints and body systems adapt to allow for more effective learning and progress not only in the early years, but even more importantly, in the adult years. When coupled with some light weight training, mainly to learn how to do the various exercises and to gain some additional strength, the results are even more dramatic.

As you become involved in different activities, your growth patterns will be enhanced, especially if your nutrition is good at this time. Understand that nutrition is the basis for development of all of the body systems, physical abilities and learning. If you do not have the needed nutrients in the body, it will not be able to adapt and make the necessary bodily changes to allow for the best growth and development.

It is possible to find good athletes who have poor nutrition, even from the very earliest years. They live mainly on pizza, candy, chips, burgers, etc., rather than wholesome, beneficial foods. Because of this, nutrition is not considered to be important by many athletes. What they fail to comprehend is that they can be much better with good nutrition. Rather than equating poor nutrition with good performance, think in terms of how great you could be with proper and effective nutrition. Keep in mind that most, if not all, athletes can be better, including professional ones.

Being good at more than one sport is beneficial in multiyear and yearly training programs. Understand that you cannot play at a high level in one sport on a year-round basis; you must take a break from your sport to allow your body (and especially your mind) to recuperate and prepare for the next intense season. When you are skilled and have the physical abilities to play another sport well, it becomes a means of maintaining your fitness without doing serious training in the off-season. The second sport will be relaxing and enjoyable when you are able to play on a high level.

Sadly, the day of the two- and three-letter athlete is coming to an end in the U.S. In previous years it was common to find all-American athletes in more than one sport. Today, however, coaches believe you must spend more time in one sport in order to become better. Thus we see an aggressive push for greater specialization from the earliest years, with little to no exposure to other great sports.

Figure 2.3: Track

But when you expose a youngster to different sports he may find one to which he is more suited or that is more appealing to him. The more he enjoys the sport, the more inclined he will be to train hard to become better in it. There will be less chance of burn-out, as often occurs when starting at an early age.

In the early stages of learning and practicing exercises for strength and endurance, you do not train like a bodybuilder or the way most personal trainers advocate, by doing three or more sets of 10, or eight to 12 repetitions. At this time, one set for 15-20 repetitions is more than sufficient since you should be doing approximately 20-25 exercises in one session. This enhances the learning and developmental process until the exercises are truly mastered and strength firmly established.

With this regime, you develop strength and muscular endurance, the two prerequisites for more intense training. Starting off by doing more sets and only a few repetitions and exercises leads to soreness and overtraining. In addition, you do not fully develop all the muscles and joints.

With this background, when you become a teenager or get past puberty and start serious training, you will have the ability to do the same and other exercises and do them well. As a result, you will make very fast progress in further improving your physical abilities and sports skills. Other key factors that are improved at this time include agility, flexibility, power, speed-strength, muscular endurance, cardiovascular endurance and reaction time.

Beginning serious training at ages 3 to 7 (except when needed) is often a waste of time and money. If you wait until the appropriate age to learn skills (which is about 10 to 11) and to develop the ability to do the skills well in the following years, the learning and enhancement of the skills are much faster.

For example, at ages 2 to 8 you do not have the necessary prerequisites of strength, flexibility, endurance or even the psychological factors of concentration and perseverance to effectively learn skills. If you had a child practice one sport from ages 2 to 8, and you had an 8-year-old who had been playing a variety of sports begin the same process, it may take the latter only a few months to develop the skills that it took the younger person five or six years to develop.

The secret in the first five- to eight-year phase of a multiyear training program is to avoid becoming regimented, as happens when you specialize in one sport. With greater exposure to many different sports and skills you become a much better athlete when you specialize later. Because you learned how to learn, it enables you to pick up and master many auxiliary factors that are impossible to get without a broad background.

Sports are constantly evolving and becoming more complex. To get an edge on what the sport will be like in 10 or 15 years, you must have the ability to learn. In this way you develop an advantage over other athletes in developing the skills needed to play on the highest levels.

II. Specialization

In the specialization phase, you become serious about your sport. You become a true, bona fide athlete, willing to train and work hard to improve your technical, physical and game skills in order to excel. The fun and games concept no longer applies. In serious training, you derive great enjoyment and satisfaction from your accomplishments and progress, especially when playing against others. Since the level of play is higher, your abilities and achievements must be greater.

The main purpose of this phase is to hone your skills to a sharp point. At the same time you fully develop the physical qualities that are involved in execution of the skills and game play.

The physical training at this time is more intense. In early training, you developed the basic body systems which can now be taxed to their limits to further improve them and tailor them to your sport. You reach adult standards in many aspects of your growth and development so that you can withstand heavier and more intense training fairly well.

To prevent overtraining, you should be monitored very closely. Many hormones are peaking at and after puberty and there is a tendency to get involved in many different activities. Thus not only must your sports activities be monitored, but also your extracurricular activities. Most important at this time is that you get ample sleep. Because of the heavy training, you require a minimum of eight to 10 hours of sleep a day! This is extremely important, as is good nutrition. Poor habits in one or both of these areas lead to decreased development and performance.

During the phase of specialization you not only focus on one sport but also train using specialized strength and explosive exercises that duplicate the techniques (muscle and joint actions) seen in execution of the sports skills and game play. Thus, you physically prepare the body and master the skills that are involved, while competing more often to display these talents and to determine what is lacking in game play. There is some competition in the very early years but it is more of a fun nature. In the phase of specialization, the competition is much more meaningful and intense.

At the end of this phase you are ready to participate on a collegiate, professional or Olympic-level team. Training continues with greater coupling of technique with your physical abilities to be able to play on these higher levels and to become an even better performer.

III. Competition

In the phase of competition you are involved in organized league play with other individuals or teams. You continue participation for as many years as you are capable and playing well enough to make a contribution to the team. In college this is usually four years but in professional sports it can be well into your 40s as seen in baseball, football, archery and track and field. As you get older, the training becomes even more important in order to keep your body and physical abilities at a level commensurate with the game play of younger players.

The following is an example of how the transition takes place from one phase to the next.

In the subteen group (9 to 13 years of age) the purpose of training is to achieve all-around physical development and mastery of a large repertoire of movements. Up to 80 percent of the training is in general physical development and approximately 20 percent in the main sport.

In the junior youth group (14 to 15 years of age), which has a high work capacity, the athlete continues all-around physical training but the ratio of general and sports-specific physical preparation changes. At this time up to 60-70 percent of the work is devoted to general physical preparation and 30-40 percent to the specific sport.

The period from 15 to 16 years of age (the senior youth group) is a transitional stage during which there is active formation of the growing body. There is usually an increase in body weight and some stabilization of growth. At this time the amount of strength training is carefully regulated and there is an increase in technical training. The main tasks at this time are the development of character and workouts in daily training sessions. In general, 50 percent of this group's work is for general physical development, 25 percent is specialized (in relation to physical preparation for the sport) and 25 percent is on technical preparation, that is, specific skill learning and improvement.

At 17 to 18 years of age the main task is organizing the training process. The quantity and type of strength training, flexibility training, agility, speed, explosiveness, etc., must be worked out for each sport and for each athlete. Especially important at this time are good nutrition and the ability of the body to recover from the training loads.

In the sub-adult age (19 to 20 years of age) the main tendencies are to further increase the training loads, especially in regard to quality and intensity. This is the main stage in the preparation of the body for highly intense and vigorous competition.

In essence, the youth years should be considered a preparatory stage whose main purpose is to build strong foundations for sports progress later in life. This means that each of these age groups is used to prepare the athlete for the training that takes place in the next youth group (phase of training). Thus, all the training is done to prepare the body for the next type of training before reaching the highest levels of competition.

IV. The Transitional Phase

After the competitive years you transition back into society so that you do not experience any great emotional or psychological setbacks in the process. This is why it is important to have an education or other interests and skills so that you have something to fall back on when you are no longer playing. Some athletes are so intent on playing that they cannot live without it. This is especially true of athletes who hope to play on professional levels but cannot make the team. Thus, care must be taken in such cases to ease back into society without serious psychological or sociological problems.

Figure 2.4: Back to society

NOTES:

Chapter 3
Posture

Posture is closely related to balance, as you must balance your body in different positions both dynamically and statically in order to achieve a particular posture. Thus, in many cases posture and balance can be one and the same. However, when you are in good balance, you may or may not be in good posture.

Many factors associated with posture must be addressed independently, as they are not directly related to balance. For example, posture affects how well you perform a sports activity, how tall you grow and how well your internal organs function for overall health and sports performance.

Do not think of posture as a military position in which you stand straight and hold a rigid position. Posture is dynamic in that you must develop the ability to assume and maintain good posture during a sports performance.

For example, having poor posture can cause structural changes in your body shape which can negatively affect your sports performance. Postural problems can lead to muscle imbalances, joint and muscle weaknesses and a loss of flexibility. As a result, you can experience neck, shoulder and back pain and, in many cases, an inability to perform as needed. Because of this, you must pay attention to posture from very early on, when the body is still in its formative stages.

When I was in school, from elementary through college, analysis of posture and exercises to correct it were strongly emphasized. Since that time posture has been mostly ignored. As a result, one can find many individuals, including athletes, who have poor posture. This includes a forward head, rounded or sloping shoulders, excessively rounded upper backs (kyphosis), hyperextension of the lower spine (sway back), hyperextended knees, toes pointed excessively outward or inward, thighs rotated excessively inward or outward, and others. These postural problems can have a strong negative effect on your sports performance.

Good posture is important to your health, because it helps to keep the internal organs in place and allows them to work efficiently and effectively. For example, if you have swayback (when the lower back is excessively arched), the intestines, instead of being held in place, press against the floor of the abdominal cavity, which interferes with their normal work. If you have rounded shoulders and an excessively rounded upper back, the chest cage becomes constricted and the lungs cannot fill adequately with air, which is vital for maximum oxygen utilization.

Dynamic and static posture is related to back problems, a common ailment in sports. Correcting the posture is often all that is needed to relieve back pain. For example, pulling the head back into proper alignment is sufficient to produce the normal curvature of the vertebral column. By lifting the head and looking forward, you can activate the lower back muscles to hold the spine in place, and as a result, perform better in skills such as running.

Strength and flexibility exercises play a very important role in attaining and maintaining good posture. For example, if you have tight hip flexors, they may keep the pelvis tilted forward, causing swayback. If the hip flexors

Figure 3.1: Back raise

are weak or if the hamstrings are too tight, it may lead to flattening of the spine. Doing exercises such as the classic lunge, good morning, back raise and squat can alleviate such problems.

When the abdominals are too tight (usually from doing too many crunches), they flatten the spine, which places excessive pressure on the anterior aspects of the spinal discs. If the abdominals are too weak, the abdomen protrudes and encourages swayback. In such cases, doing full-range abdominal exercises such as Yessis Back Machine (glute-ham) sit-ups and back raises are beneficial.

Having weak or overstretched upper back muscles, as often occurs from too much bench pressing or too many crunches, usually leads to excessively stretched upper back muscles, which in turn leads to rounded shoulders and tight chest muscles. A forward head, on the other hand, is usually caused by weak muscles in the back of the neck as well as habitual practices such as sitting at a desk or reading or writing for many hours without counteracting the forward head position. Specific exercises to strengthen the muscles involved and to stretch some of the tight muscles are then needed to regain more effective posture.

Figure 3.2: Back stretch with the back stretch strap

Participation in sports does not lead to significant improvements in posture. In some cases, especially if your skill technique is poor, it can lead to additional problems or exacerbate pre-existing ones. To prevent musculoskeletal injuries and to gain effective posture require a good exercise program and good alignment when standing, sitting, walking, running and doing other activities. Good posture should become a habit.

For example, if you have rounded shoulders, your arms may be slightly in front of the body instead of hanging alongside it. As a result, you may find that instead of lifting the arms directly overhead, you lift them in front of the body, which can create excessive stress on the shoulders, especially when done against resistance. Or it may force you to cross the midline of the body when running.

If you cannot hold your trunk erect while running, you will be unable to have an effective push-off or knee drive for optimal stride length. If your feet or thighs are rotated outward excessively, it places great stress on the hip and knee joints and can lead to injury.

Improper alignment results in additional muscular effort and strain, especially since it creates rotary moments at the various joints. If the excess muscular effort is sufficient to produce fatigue, it can eventually affect your technique and total performance. In more severe cases, the strain on the joints can be sufficient to alter structure. There is also evidence to indicate that chronic strain contributes to arthritic types of ailments in later life.

The spine is the keystone of the body structure. It must support the weight of the head, trunk and upper extremities. In addition, it is the solid point of attachment for most of the muscles, anchoring and controlling the pectoral shoulder girdle as well as the latissimus dorsi and other muscles of the back which move the arm. These functions require a strong, well-supported spinal unit.

Because of this, the spine should be a firm, carefully articulated and not-too-flexible column. In essence, you should be able to maintain the four natural curves of the spine at all times during sports performance and when not exercising. The most important exercise you can do to achieve and maintain spinal alignment is the back raise.

Seemingly small, insignificant deviations in posture can lead to major changes in the body. For example, if your feet are not sufficiently strong to keep the body balanced and the shins in line with the feet, it can change the positioning of the knees, which in turn, affect the hips, which in turn, affect the spine, which will then affect the head position. Each joint will then be limited in the actions it is capable of performing, especially when the deviation is coupled with tight muscles on one side and weak muscles on the other.

Balancing one's weight has a very definite bearing on the feet. How the legs are used in activities such as running is directly influenced by the joints, ligaments and muscles in the limbs above it. Thus any problems in the lower body will affect the upper body, and vice versa.

Last but not least, good posture makes you feel good. Because of its many benefits, including ease of movement, good balance of muscle strength and flexibility, proper positioning of the spine and proper functioning of the internal organs, good posture makes the body feel good. When you possess good posture you are proud of yourself and ready to perform. Thus, posture should be a prime focus in your program.

Improving Height

There is a straight-line relationship between posture, sports performance and increasing body height. In training there is improved circulation and respiration, neuro-hormonal regulation, intensification of the exchange processes and an increase in growth hormones. As a result, there is stimulation of the muscles, blood vessels, ligaments, tendons and bones—in a word, harmonious growth of the entire body including upward growth.

In dynamic stretching the long bones in the growth zones are lightened; that is, the active cells are not as compacted after the stretching. As a result, the cells multiply within the growth zone and serve to increase the length of the bones. The key is to perform exercises on a regular basis that not only help stretch the spine and maintain the normal curvature, but also increase the growth of the individual long tubular bones.

Your height over the day changes. In the morning it is possible to be one quarter to one inch taller than in the evening. This is tied to the height of the spinal column, which is not a firm vertical post but a resilient, elastic, pivoting rod having four curves. Because there are curves, the actual length of the spinal column from the head to the tailbone is less than its length if it was fully extended and straightened. The more expressed each of the curves is, the less is your height. The difference between a curved and a straight spine can be greater than three to four inches.

In the morning when the muscles have good tone, height is greater than at night when the muscles are fatigued, resulting in larger spinal curves. In essence, the trunk "caves in" and becomes shorter. The muscles play an important role as they also bend the spine. As the tightness of the muscles increases, it leads to a tightening of the curves and, as a result, height decreases by one or more inches. In the evening if you stretch and stand tall, height will increase. Some circus performers are capable of increasing their height by seven inches. They relax and tighten specific muscles to straighten the spine and increase height, and to become shorter they merely increase the curves.

Thus, if you are interested in increasing your height you should first of all pay attention to improving posture. Strengthen the muscles of the body, especially those that maintain the vertical position of the spine. Most important here are midsection exercises such as the back raise, back raise with a twist, reverse trunk twist, reverse sit-ups, Yessis Machine (glute-ham) sit-ups, and stretches such as inversion (hanging on a high bar with full relaxation of the body) and the full back stretch with the Back Stretch Strap.

Jumps for maximum height, striving to reach a high-hanging object, are effective stimulants for the growth zone of the bones. Doing many jumps throughout the day whenever an opportunity arises is excellent. Even hanging from the branch of a tree when out for a walk or hanging and swinging from a high bar, followed by more jumping are all excellent activities.

Physical exercises have a strong physiological effect on your body. Most important is the intensification of the exchange processes which serve to increase the mass of the bone tissues in the period of growth and formation of the young body. Especially effective for growth are the loads placed on the bones which have a dynamic and pulsating character.

The key to maximizing growth is to get maximum relaxation of the muscles followed by strengthening of the muscles. When you stretch you unload the growth centers in the bones and fully extend the spine. Strengthening the muscles after the spine or bones have been elongated helps to lock them into this position. As a result, these exercises increase height and improve posture.

NOTES:

Chapter 4
Mastery of Technique

Based on theory and practical experiences, the best way to improve athletically and become a high-level athlete is to fully develop skill technique and the physical abilities that relate to skill execution. Technique must be constantly worked on during the early years and throughout the years as you develop more of your physical abilities. You must constantly modify your technique execution in relation to increases in strength, agility, flexibility, explosiveness and power. Development of only technique or only physical attributes will improve your performance to a limited extent. The most dramatic increases are seen when your physical abilities are coupled with technique.

Figure 4.1: Beach volleyball, going for a dig

Figure 4.2: Tennis forehand

For example, I helped train a professional beach volleyball player. She wanted to be quicker, faster and more explosive. At that time, she was ranked in the 20s in the U.S., in the 30s internationally. She was an all-American in college and played volleyball in Europe. She did weight and other forms of training during college and in Europe.

After evaluating her abilities I saw significant room for improvement. I put her on a specialized technique, strength and explosive training program. After analyzing her game films, moves to enhance her quickness were introduced and strength and flexibility exercises specific to these new movements were created. As a result of doing these exercises, her abilities on the court improved greatly. She had never seen exercises like the ones that I prescribed for her, but she was very familiar with weight training exercises. When she saw how the exercises related specifically to what she did on the court, she became even more interested in her workouts.

In one year her rankings in the U.S. and internationally dropped over 10 places. She is still making progress and her team is now ranked as the number 3-5 seed nationally and 9-15 internationally. Even though she is 6 foot 4 inches tall, she is very quick on the court, has a good vertical jump and powerful spikes. The same can happen to you when you improve your technique and the physical abilities specific to your technique.

In sports such as golf, only recently has the training of physical abilities begun to play a major role. For many years golfers relied mainly on technique and equipment for improvement. But there is no consensus among golf instructors as to what constitutes an effective swing. An editor of one of the major golf magazines was proud of the fact that there was so much diversity among the teaching professionals in regard to what constituted good technique. This is why each issue of the magazine contains articles that are contradictory.

However, not having a consensus as to what constitutes effective technique means that the pros do not understand the technique that they teach! Instead they perpetuate a lot of B.S. to appear as experts. In this context B.S. is used to indicate that what the person says is neither the truth nor a lie. There is usually little concern for whether it is true or not. Also, B.S. is usually found whenever someone must speak on a topic that exceeds his knowledge or expertise.

For examples of good technique we seem to rely on what high-level or world-class performers do or say they do in the execution of their skills. Since they are the world's best, it is assumed that they have the best technique and know what they do in skill execution. This cannot be further from the truth! A classic example of this was brought out in the 1980s when Thomas and Brumel were exchanging the world record in the high jump for many years.

In execution of the jump it was noted that Brumel (a Soviet athlete) raised his right arm as he dove over the bar (roll-over technique). The experts thought it was odd that he should be driving the arm up, not down. When Thomas (a U.S. athlete) was asked whether he also did this, he emphatically stated that he drove his arm down, not up, as he dove over the bar. This seemed logical; you would want to drive the arm down on the side that was going over the bar to help the body and trail leg roll over.

In reality, raising the arm up as the body was passing over the bar created a contra-ipsolateral effect by which raising the right arm automatically helped raise the left, trailing leg. This helped to get the leg over the bar to make clearance easier. When Thomas was filmed and his movements analyzed, it was noted that he also raised the arm, but not to the same extent. Thus, even though he swore that he drove the arm down, in reality he drove it up, showing that he did not truly understand what he did in the execution of the jump.

Many other examples can be given of how technique, for the most part, is not closely examined. But once you understand that there is a commonality among sports skills and you grasp the basics of the general skill, you will be able to develop other sports skills. When technique is not fully understood it is usually made more complicated when taught. This is not intentional, it's a consequence of the lack of knowledge.

In the following chapters you will see descriptions and explanations of the basic skills of running, jumping, throwing, hitting and kicking. Once you understand how each skill is executed and how you can improve, it will make you a better athlete in all sports that require the skill. You do not change the skill because you are in a different sport – except for some minor changes. Once you learn the basic skills, you can use the same basic neuromuscular skill pattern in other sports. For example, the jumping action is the same in sports such as basketball, volleyball, soccer, football and the high jump. If you learn to jump well, you can excel in these sports when it comes to jumping for maximum height.

In some cases, you may need an approach run, as in the track-and-field jumps and the driving lay-up in basketball, but the jump is the same. It does not matter whether you are rebounding or jumping to execute a shot or to catch a ball in the air. You may do different things with the hands and body as you go up in the air, or the time of execution may vary, but the jump execution is the same.

There are also great similarities between swinging a baseball bat and a golf club in regard to weight shift, hip and shoulder rotation, shoulder actions and wrist break. Even the tennis forehand is very similar to baseball batting. There are, of course, some differences but the patterns are the same, and once you master one, it becomes relatively easy to master the other.

Kicking is another excellent example of an action that is the same regardless of the sport. This is the reason it is not uncommon to see soccer players now playing football executing field goals and point-after kicks and kick-offs.

It is because of these similarities and common movement patterns in the various sports that youngsters should learn all of the basic movement patterns. This should be done in the youth leagues and in the elementary and high schools. However, because "fun" is usually more important, the skills are skimmed over and playing takes its place.

Even though learning many basic skills at an early age is often overlooked, it may become very important when you are an adult and wish to change sports or play an additional sport. For example, when Michael Jordan was playing his best in basketball, he retired and tried out for major league baseball. However, he was not a very good hitter and was soon cut. In looking at his hitting films, it

Figure 4.3: Distance runner

was obvious that he could not execute the basic movement patterns sufficiently. Even though he may have played baseball as a youngster, he never learned a good hitting pattern, and thus was unable to achieve success as an adult in baseball. But he could have learned how to hit well if someone had taught him the basic movement pattern.

Many years ago, I received an award for best all-around athlete. I played almost every sport that was available, and whenever I saw a new sport I had to play it. As a result, I was soon able to master a sport in relatively little time because I had the abilities and the basic movement patterns for the new sport already developed. It was only a matter of adjusting the skills to the new sport.

When you are able to do this, you will find that all sports are very enjoyable. I am always amazed when people talk about how one sport is better than another. All sports can offer an equal amount of enjoyment! The key is being able to successfully execute the basic skill patterns. When someone says that he or she does not enjoy a sport, you will almost always find that he or she does not have the skills to play well.

Skill execution does not change between players. *Everyone must execute the same actions in order to execute the skill effectively.* The only differences between players are seen in range of motion, the sequence of the body parts going into action, the speed with which the limbs are moved, and the number of body parts involved. In other words, even though everyone does the same thing, they can all express it somewhat differently. This is why executing the same skill may look different to the naked eye.

Once you understand and master the basic actions involved in each skill, you will be able to play almost any sport and play it well. Keep in mind that in addition to learning and perfecting technique, if you also improve your physical abilities as they relate to your technique, it will make you much better. All of this is very possible.

Learning Sports Skills

Because youngsters are not brought up with skill learning, they just want to go out and play for "fun." They will laugh, make fun of others and fool around, especially when another player has poor skills. But they will not truly enjoy the sport. Few teachers, players and coaches realize that technique and physical learning — which also has a strong mental component — are basically the same as learning English, math, biology, etc.

There are no shortcuts to learning the basic skills, regardless of age. The speed with which you learn a skill varies greatly. However, the greater your level of development of the various physical qualities, especially strength, the faster and more effectively you can learn.

Learning motor skills is a complex physiological process. Without going into great detail, the following is a very simplified explanation of the mental and physical processes that take place. To initiate the process you should first observe the skill as it is executed. The more accurately the instructor demonstrates the skill, the more effectively you will perceive the actions involved. This is why the instructor's initial demonstration must be excellent!

Initial learning may also come from a verbal explanation of what should be done. This is effective for adults or more skilled players, but is not suitable for the very young who learn by imitating actions.

Upon viewing a clear demonstration, physiological changes occur in the body, especially if you have been concentrating on the presentation. As the action is viewed, impulses are automatically sent from the brain to the muscles involved in executing the movement. These are very subtle signals that do not result in movement. But the activation of the proper brain centers together with signals going to the muscles begins.

This is how you can learn the rudiments of a skill simply from watching an athlete play. As you watch, the nervous system responds by repeatedly sending signals to the muscles. If you decide to execute the movement, the muscles can then perform the skill. It will not be a refined movement, but a very gross pattern will be visible.

After viewing the skill and hearing words that help explain the movement, you attempt the movement one or more times. You then observe the results of the actions and, with a good understanding of what should be done, automatically make some of the necessary corrections. It is at this time that an instructor should indicate what you should do to make the execution even more effective. You then continue to repeat the action with corrections, until successful execution is achieved.

The exact number of repetitions needed before you can execute a skill with some degree of reliability is hard to establish. The more complex the skill, the greater the number of repetitions. This is why learning one portion of the total skill is very effective in the early stages. Not only is it faster to learn a small part of the total skill, but you can see success sooner, which provides greater motivation to continue the learning process.

As you repeat the skill, a motor pathway is developed from the brain to the muscles, resulting in movement. During and after execution, signals picked up by the joint and muscle proprioceptors are sent back to the brain with all the details of the action. Muscle proprioceptors measure the stretch occuring in the muscle and tendons, the pressure inside the muscle, and the stretch in the muscle. When visual or verbal corrections are given to improve the movement, changes are made in the brain centers and modified signals are then sent to the muscles for refined repetitions. This process is continued until a firm motor pathway develops.

Once the neuromuscular pathway is well established, the brain becomes less involved and the execution becomes more of a reflex action. When a stimulus is given to execute the movement, it is executed automatically without any active thinking involved. However, in the initial stages of learning there is a great deal of thinking involved as there must be full concentration on executing the movement. As the skill is mastered and perfected, brain involvement can then switch to game strategy and tactics.

Once the skill becomes automatic, it is truly learned. In essence, the motor pathway that has been developed in the neuromuscular system is so well ingrained that it remains for the rest of your life. You will be able to duplicate the skill years later, even if you have not practiced it for many years. The execution will not be exactly the same because you may have developed a fear of falling or injury, experienced a loss of strength or speed, or developed slower reactions, but the basics will be there.

Learning skills should be quite simple, but for many it is difficult and frustrating. Reasons may include lack of minimum levels of coordination, lack of strength or other physical qualities or not having a strong movement background. This is why it is so important to participate in many different activities as a youngster. The greater the number of activities in which you participate, the easier it is to learn new skills and to modify or improve the skills that were learned earlier. *You gain the ability to learn, the key to achieving the highest levels of performance.*

The need for correct technique repetitions is extremely important when first learning skills and for reinforcement of the skill. However, constant repetition of the same skill is boring and you may lose interest. To avoid boredom there should be a multitude of partial skills taught on a regular basis with practice of several skills in one session. This will help keep you interested and produce more effective and complete learning of not just one skill, but many.

To assist you in the teaching and/or learning process, the following chapters contain descriptions and sequence pictures of the basic skills of running, jumping, throwing, hitting and kicking. There are sequence pictures of different-level athletes as well as athletes in different sports who use the same skills. As the learning and mastery of these sports skills become easier, adjustments can be made to incorporate new movements.

For example, running is a basic skill, but cutting (changing directions quickly while running) is a combination not only of running but also elements of stopping, starting and jumping. Possessing these skills makes it possible to execute the cutting actions faster and more effectively.

NOTES:

Chapter 5
Running

Basic running technique (form) is the same for all athletes regardless of speed. The actions of the running leg include ankle extension, and forward (flexion) and backward (extension) movement of the thighs. The trunk remains erect with the head directly over the shoulders, the shoulders directly above the hips, and the eyes focused in front. The arm action consists of forward and backward movement from the shoulders. See Cinematograms 5.1, 5.2, 5.3 and 5.4.

There are three phases of running: the push-off, flight and touchdown. The main action in the push-off is ankle joint extension. See Cinematogram 5.1, Frames 3-5 and Cinematogram 5.3, Frames 3-4. There is some straightening of the push-off leg (knee extension) but not to full extension. See Cinematogram 5.1, Frame 4 and Cinematogram 5.2, Frame 4. Simultaneous to the push-off, the swing leg thigh is driven forward until it comes up to approximately a 45- to 90-degree angle to the vertical. The exact height of the thigh is determined by the force of the forward knee drive, which, in turn, is based on the running speed.

For example, a marathon runner's thigh rises to approximately a 45-degree angle, while a sprinter's thigh is closer to the 75- to 90-degree angle. See Cinematogram 5.1, Frame 4, of a sprinter whose thigh is driven up to 70-

80 degrees and Cinematogram 5.2, Frames 4-5, of a long-distance runner whose thigh rises to 45-60 degrees. Slow runners and joggers raise the thigh to about a 30-degree angle while some barely bring the thigh forward from the body at all. The latter is considered an example of poor technique and can be referred to as shuffling rather than true running. This running is seen most often in ultramarathoners and near the end of a marathon when runners are tired.

After the push-off foot breaks contact with the ground, the flight phase begins. At this time the push-off leg continues moving backward and bends in the knee joint as the thigh begins forward movement. As a result the shin is level to the ground or slightly higher than level as the thigh swings forward. See Cinematogram 5.1, Frames 6-8, and Cinematogram 5.2, Frames

Cinematogram 5.1: Sprinter

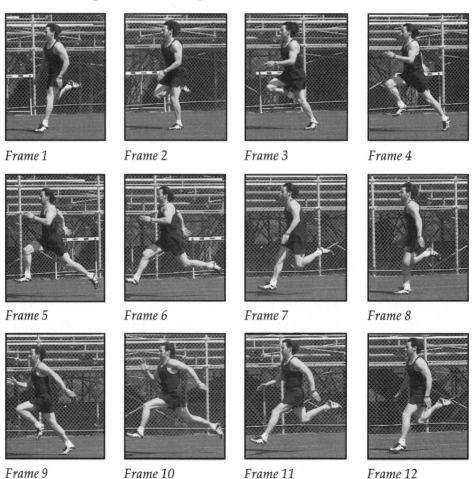

Frame 1   Frame 2   Frame 3   Frame 4

Frame 5   Frame 6   Frame 7   Frame 8

Frame 9   Frame 10   Frame 11   Frame 12

6-8. When the knee is in front of the body, the leg extends while the thigh remains up or drops slightly (see Cinematogram 5.1, Frames 5-6, and Cinematogram 5.2, Frames 4-6), and is then brought backward and downward in a pawback (pullback) action. The pawback is best seen in 5.1, Frames 6-8.

The faster the leg is moving backward when ground contact is made (touchdown phase), the lower are the forward braking forces and the more the upper body is moved forward. This, in turn, makes the following push-off more effective since it will be in a more horizontal direction rather than vertical, as occurs when the push-off takes place with the upper body over or just slightly in front of the support leg. This typically occurs with heel hitters, when touchdown occurs on the heel of the foot rather than the midfoot or ball-heel.

The greatest separation between both legs occurs in the flight phase. The angle measured between the forward and backward thighs of sprinters is usually about 140-160 degrees (see 5.1, Frame 5). In slower runners it is considerably less, often about 30-45 degrees.

Cinematogram 5.2: Long Distance Runner

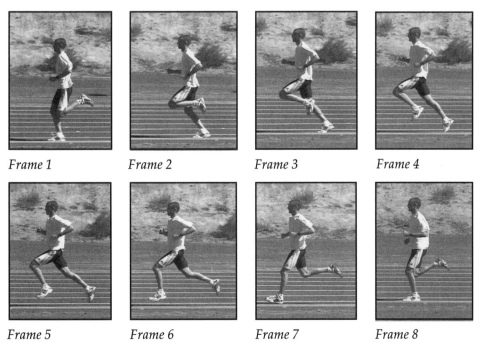

Frame 1   Frame 2   Frame 3   Frame 4

Frame 5   Frame 6   Frame 7   Frame 8

In sprinting, as the forward leg is brought backward, the foot makes contact with the ground on the ball of the foot or midfoot. For some runners touchdown is on the anterior (forward) portion of the heel, closest to the arch, and on the lateral border or on the entire foot. The latter, however, is more common in long-distance running. In such touchdowns the arch of the foot is capable of absorbing some of the landing forces. The Achilles tendon and calf muscles undergo great tension by withstanding the landing forces and prepare them for a forceful push-off.

When touchdown is made farther out in front of the body, first contact is made on the heel of the foot, which creates braking forces that impede forward progress. Landing on the heel with the sole of the foot angled upward is inefficient and can be highly dangerous. The forces encountered can be very high (over 10 times body weight), and if experienced over a long period of time, cause ankle, knee, hip and even lower-back problems. Despite this, it appears that the heel hit continues to be recommended by coaches, and shoe companies advocate cushioned heels for heel strikers so that they can continue this ineffective form of running.

Cinematogram 5.3: Sprinter

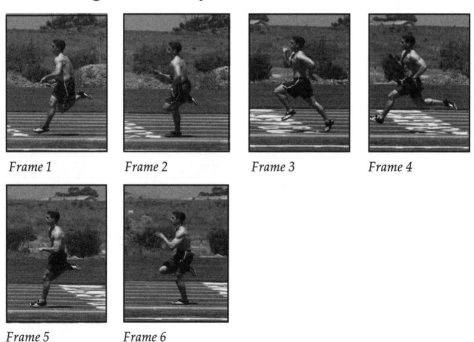

Frame 1   Frame 2   Frame 3   Frame 4

Frame 5   Frame 6

One indicator of good running technique is to see only one thigh during touchdown when observing from the side. When the backward moving leg makes contact with the ground, the thigh of the forward swing leg lines up opposite the support leg. In other words, when looking from the side you see only one leg for an instant. This is more easily seen on videotape when viewed frame by frame. See Cinematogram 5.1, Frame 1 and Cinematogram 5.2, Frame 1. Note that in Cinematogram 5.3, Frame 2, the sprinter has already driven the thigh forward of the support leg. This is excellent sprint technique as it helps increase speed.

The running technique described is applicable to adults, runners who are 11 years of age and older. From ages 6-11, youngsters usually do not

Cinematogram 5.4: Youngster Sprinting

Frame 1   Frame 2   Frame 3   Frame 4

Frame 5   Frame 6   Frame 7   Frame 8

Frame 9   Frame 10   Frame 11   Frame 12

have the coordination or muscle strength to execute good technique. In fact running technique in most children is very inefficient. Those who have greater strength or effective instruction usually do better.

For example, if you look at Cinematogram 5.4 of a 9-year-old runner, you will see some of the inefficient movements. He does have some excellent aspects to his run. For example, he has a great push-off as can be seen in Frames 1-2. However, the ankle action is still not strong and is not using the full range of motion, as can be seen in Frame 3. Rather than having a strong pawback action, he drops his thigh quickly to make contact with the ground in Frames 2-6. The landing, however, is in good position, only slightly in front and under the body.

Cinematogram 5.5: Middle Distance Runner

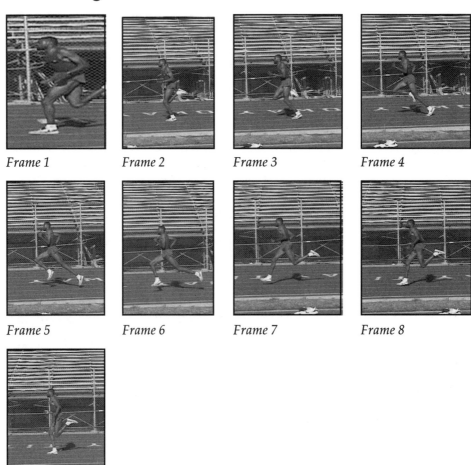

Frame 1   *Frame 2*   *Frame 3*   *Frame 4*

Frame 5   *Frame 6*   *Frame 7*   *Frame 8*

Frame 9

He has good erect posture, although he carries his shoulders a little too high and there is stiffness in the upper body. In addition, there is excessive rotation of the shoulders, all of which are indicative of striving to run as fast as possible, but without the ability to change at this age. If the coach working with him now is correcting some of these aspects, this youngster can be an outstanding runner. He currently plays Pop Warner football and his speed has enabled him to become a good player, but if he is to be great in high school and college, he will need changes in his technique and further improvement in his physical abilities.

Regardless of age, one of the most important things a runner can do is to strengthen the hip, abdominal and lower-back muscles. These are important for stabilizing the pelvis, allowing for proper thigh movement, and moving the legs at a faster rate. Typically, most runners will have a fairly good push-off but lack a strong knee drive forward and pawback.

For example, look at Cinematogram 5.5. These are sequential pictures of a three-time Olympian in the 800 and 1500 meters. He is a gold and silver medalist, not only in the Olympics but also in the World Championships. If you look at Frame 1, you can see that the landing is in front of the body and the swing leg has not driven forward as quickly as possible. When you can see only one thigh, he has already begun his push-off. The knee has driven sufficiently forward and he has had a great push-off with exceptionally long legs. This has been the key to his success in running.

However, he does not have very strong ankle extension and his pawback is lacking. Look at Frames 7, 8 and 9; you can see how the entire leg is not brought back forcefully, but instead he bends the knee slightly to make contact with the ground quickly. If he had made some of these changes, he might have been more successful in his chances to compete a fourth time in the Olympic games. As it was, he kept breaking down with injuries, mainly because he did not do any strength training (which could have helped his technique). Understand that special strength training becomes even more important as you age.

One of the most common errors made by runners is a lack of pawback action. This movement occurs after you drive the leg forward and then drive it down and backward to make contact with the ground. Understand that running speed consists of driving the leg forward and driving the leg backward. These two actions give you up to 80% of the total force generated for producing speed. Ankle extension provides the remainder during hte push-off. Almost all runners have a fairly effective push-off and knee drive or thigh swinging forward movement, but lack the pawback action. When it is present, it is usually weak.

Mastering the pawback movement, however, is not always easy. Many athletes and runners seem to have difficulty with this action, probably because they are accustomed to bringing the knee forward and then straight down to contact the ground slightly in front of the body. In other cases, they land with the foot well out in front of the body on the heel.

One of the best exercises to develop the feel of the pawback movement is known as circling or wheeling in which your foot circumscribes a circle. To execute, assume a standing position, raise the thigh upward until it is almost level and hold it up as you reach out with the lower leg until the leg is straight. Then drive the straight leg down and back so that the foot hits directly underneath the body. Do this with one leg for four to five repetitions to ge tthe feel of the actions and then do it with the opposite leg.

For many athletes, the pawback movement is a new feeling, especially if they have been landing heel first. When you recognize what the landing should feel like, then when you execute pawback you will have a better understanding of how it should feel when the foot touches down in an effective run. Most runners experience a springy action and feel that the landing is much lighter and easier when they land midfoot or ball-heel. You will find your running at this time easier and you will feel light-footed. You will feel yourself moving faster with less effort — the key to effective running, especially for speed.

Fluid thigh movement forward and backward is important for effective running. It is necessary to eliminate angled thigh movements, such as criss-crossing of the legs. It is not uncommon to see the thighs (knees) cross the midline of the body, usually due to limited strength of the midsection rotational muscles which allow the hips to rotate excessively, as well as to weak hip muscle strength to stabilize the hips. To compensate, the shoulders then rotate to counteract the hip rotation.

Many runners have a tendency to sink low on the support leg (squat) during touchdown. This can be corrected by developing greater eccentric and isometric strength of the leg muscles so that they can hold a straighter leg. This keeps you taller and limits the amount of vertical (up and down) movements which are very inefficient.

The hip flexor muscles drive the thigh forward and upward and the extensors bring the leg down and back to make contact with the ground. Once the leg is in full support, the upper body should be over the foot or slightly in front of the support leg. When the push-off begins, the upper body should be well forward of the support leg so that the push-off will have a strong horizontal force component and allow you to run more level to the ground (see Cinematograms 5.1, 5.2 and 5.3).

The arm action in running is closely synchronized to the leg action. Also, the range of motion exhibited in the shoulder joints is usually equal to the range of motion seen in the hip joints. Because of the close coordination between the arms and legs, the arms serve a very valuable purpose in balancing movements of the legs to provide for more effective running technique.

The arm action stabilizes the shoulders, keeps them in a front-facing position during the run. When you have good form, the arm action is basically forward and backward and there is very little shoulder rotation. This action helps to stabilize the pelvis so that the leg action is more directly to the front and rear.

If the shoulders rotate greatly, the hips would then rotate to counteract the shoulders to keep the body in a front facing position. Doing this is very energy inefficient. When the shoulders rotate, the arms will appear to cross the body. But they will still be "forward and backward" in relation to the shoulder angle. If the hips were allowed to rotate to the left and right to produce a longer stride length, you would run in a zigzag pattern rather than straight ahead.

In long-distance running, the elbows remain bent at approximately a right angle throughout the run (see Cinematogram 5.2). This arm positioning creates a short lever (shoulder to elbow), making it easier to swing the arms with less energy. This is efficient for long-distance running, but in sprinting the arms do not act merely as pendulums but coordinate precisely with the leg action. During the pawback when the leg is being brought down and back for touchdown, the arm straightens in a downward direction, creating more downward force. As the foot makes full contact, the arm extends (is driven down) and

Cinematogram 5.6: Glute-ham-gastroc raise

Frame 1   *Frame 2*   *Frame 3*

creates a greater ground reaction force. See Cinematogram 5.1, Frames 6-8, for full arm extension and Cinematogram 5.3, Frame 2, for partial straightening.

The straightened arm synchronizes with the support phase of the leg. As the leg prepares for push-off, the elbow of the straightened arm is brought up to the rear, creating a 90-degree angle in the elbow. When the swing leg is driven forward, the arm comes through very quickly with a shortened lever to synchronize with the knee drive for more forward force.

Some of the best specialized strength and flexibility exercises that you can do to improve your running are:

1. Heel raises to improve the ankle joint extension in the push-off.

2. Squats and slow delay squats to stay "tall" and to keep from sinking too low during the support phase.

3. Knee drive with Active Cords to improve the knee drive.

4. Hip extension (pawback) with Active Cords to have a more powerful pull-back action.

5. Good Morning and glute-ham-gastroc raises for greater strength of the hamstrings and a more powerful pawback (Cinematogram 5.6).

6. Back raises to help maintain the upright, erect trunk position.

In addition to these exercises, you should do lead-up plyometric exercises such as hopping, jumping and skipping, to develop muscle resiliency. You will then be ready for more explosive exercises to further increase speed. See chapter 19 and my book *Explosive Running* for details.

As you do specialized strength and flexibility exercises for running, you should see significant improvement in your running technique and speed. In addition, as your physical abilities specific to your running technique improve, you will be ready to take on more advanced forms of training. This is especially important for sprinters. If you are a long-distance runner, then the exercises mentioned above may be sufficient to improve and to maintain your abilities. However, you should also do other running-specific exercises to get better all-around development and to help prevent injury.

To learn more about these exercises, read *Explosive Running*. Not only does it go into detailed technique analysis of running at different speeds, but it also includes all the major exercises that you can do to improve your technique, running abilities and speed. The exercises are described in detail and illustrated with photographs.

NOTES:

Chapter 6
Jumping

The ability to jump well is needed in many different sports. For example, in basketball, jump height is critical not only for executing a good jump shot but also for rebounding and blocking shots. In volleyball, jump height is essential for executing the best spike and for effective blocking. Events such as the high jump and long jump in track and field require different kinds of jumps, but the same basic take-off mechanisms are involved.

The ability to jump high is important when executing various head shots in soccer, when catching high-thrown balls in football and baseball, and when intercepting or blocking a pass in football. Even in swimming, jump ability is important when taking off from the blocks as well as pushing off on the turns. In diving, the higher you can jump, the more time you will have to execute different dives.

The ability to jump well is needed in explosive and speed-strength training. Many explosive (plyometric and shock) training exercises entail some form of jumping, not only with the legs but also with the arms. Thus, how well you jump is critical to your athletic performance. When you do easy jump activities such as skipping rope or simple hopping and skipping, technique is not critical. But as the jumps become more powerful, how you take off and land become extremely important for best results and injury prevention. See Cinematograms 6.1-6.4 for sequence pictures of different jumps.

Jump Technique

Stance

In the initial stance, your feet should be placed directly under your hips so that when you straighten your legs, they push the hips and upper body straight upward. If you place your feet wider than hip-width apart, when your legs extend, the forces created will cross your body. As a result, only a portion of the forces generated will be used to raise your body.

The key to an effective vertical jump is to be sure that your take-off leg(s) is under your center of gravity (hips). This is the key to moving your entire body upward as high as possible on the jump. See Cinematogram 6.1, Frame 1 and Cinematogram 6.3, Frame 1. When jumping for distance, your foot should be behind the hips as you take off to drive the hips (body) forward.

Cinematogram 6.1: Front View

Frame 1

Frame 2

Frame 3

Frame 4

Frame 5

Frame 6

Frame 7

Frame 8

Frame 9

Take-off

In effective jumping there are sequential joint extension actions in the hip, knee and ankle joints. The arms assist in gaining greater height and distance. To execute a jump, it is first necessary to go into a squat (crouch) so that there is flexion in the ankle, knee and hip joints. The trunk inclines forward and the arms are free to swing alongside the body. See Cinematogram 6.3, Frames 1-3 and Cinematogram 6.1, Frames 2-3.

In a powerful jump there is a slight but quick drop of the body, after which the trunk is raised followed by knee extension, which pushes the body upward. See Cinematogram 6.2, Frames 3-6 and Cinematogram 6.1, Frames 2-5. When the legs are almost straight, the ankles go into extension and you leave the ground with a fully extended body, with the legs straight and the toes pointed downward. See Cinematogram 6.3, Frames 6-7 and 6.1, Frames 6-7.

Frame 1

Cinematogram 6.2: Side View

Frame 2

Frame 3

Frame 4

Frame 5

Frame 6

Frame 7

Frame 8

Frame 9

For a quickly executed jump for height, the less of a crouch you take prior to the take-off the better. When you have plenty of time, a deep crouch is also effective. In the crouch, you place the extensor muscles that are used in the upward jump on eccentric stretch to develop tension. The eccentric contraction switches to an isometric contraction when the downward movement is stopped in preparation for the upward (take-off) movement. At that time the muscular contraction switches to concentric. The faster the changes in these muscular contractions take place, the higher you will jump.

Cinematogram 6.3: Side View

Frame 1   Frame 2   Frame 3   Frame 4

Frame 5   Frame 6   Frame 7   Frame 8

Frame 9   Frame 10   Frame 11   Frame 12

If the ankles and knees start first, which occurs quite often in youngsters, you will not be able to jump to your maximum height. See Cinematogram 6.2, Frames 4-6. It is important to extend the trunk first so that the upper body moves upward to the erect (vertical) position as the knees and then the ankles create the force needed to propel the body into the air. Some overlap of the joint actions takes place. It is also common to see athletes use all three joints simultaneously, but doing this produces less force.

As you prepare for the jump by going into a downward movement, the arms swing down and then up in an arc. This movement is

Cinematogram 6.4: Jump Shot

Frame 1   Frame 2   Frame 3   Frame 4

Frame 5   Frame 6   Frame 7   Frame 8

Frame 9   Frame 10   Frame 11   Frame 12

quite vigorous and places a greater load on the legs so that the muscles can respond with more force in the push-off. When the arms approach an approximately 45-degree angle in front of the body, they begin to "un-weight" the body. Depending upon the type of jump, the arms either stop when they are level with the ground or continue upward, as in a basketball or volleyball block. See Cinematogram 6.1, Frames 2-6 and Cinematogram 6.3, Frames 2-6.

To get more hang time — a momentary increase in the amount of time at the peak of the jump — athletes drive the arms downward as they approach peak height. This can be seen in Cinematograms 6.1, 6.2 and 6.3. For example, if you look closely at Cinematogram 6.1, you can see that the arms from Frames 6-9 move out and down as the jumper goes upward. Thus, when he reaches the peak with the arms going down, he has a momentary increase. This is also seen in cinematogram 6.2, Frames 6-9 and Cinematogram 6.3, Frames 6-9. But if you must execute a shot or block when you jump in the air, this movement becomes impossible. In this case there is no "extra" hang time.

If you must perform when airborne, the take-off changes slightly. In Cinematogram 6.4, you will notice that as the jumper lands, he has a slight crouch but the trunk is basically erect so that he can look upward to see where he will be shooting. Thus the jump is executed mainly via knee- and ankle-joint extension. Slight arching of the back that occurs in Frames 7-8 is more for the shooting and not to assist in the jump, because he is already airborne.

This player also relies on almost simultaneous ankle and knee action in his jump. If you look closely at Frames 5-7, you will see that there is straightening in both the knee and ankle joints occurring at the same time.

Note that this player uses a different approach from what is typically taught to athletes, especially in basketball and volleyball. Rather than use the step-together-jump technique, I taught him to take off on one leg, land on both feet and jump immediately with both legs. This jump is much quicker and gives you the same if not more height, provided you have well-developed explosive strength.

After I taught this player how to execute this jump, he saw immediate benefit when trying to get his jumpshot off quickly so it could not be blocked by his opponent. This technique may also benefit middle spikers and blockers in volleyball who must quickly jump to block or spike in order to be successful. Soccer players may also find this technique useful if they have to jump quickly for a headshot.

Landing

When preparing for touchdown, your feet should be directly under your hips so that the landing forces can be handled efficiently by the leg muscles. Landing should take place on the balls of the feet, followed immediately by the heels. This is followed in turn by ankle-, knee- and hip-joint flexion, respectively. Do not point your toes as you descend so that you land on them. This position can cause excessive jamming of the foot bones which can create foot problems.

The key to a safe and effective touchdown is to land with the underside of the foot approximately 45 degrees to the horizontal so that ball-heel or midfoot contact occurs very quickly. This allows for the arch of the foot to absorb the initial shock and to withstand most of the landing forces. This is not only the most effective form of landing, but one that will prevent injury. See Cinematogram 6.2, Frame 3.

To ensure an effective and safe landing, you should tense your foot and leg muscles slightly while you are still in the air. In other words, mentally and physically prepare for touchdown before actually making contact. When you do this, the muscles and tendons will engage more strongly as you make initial contact and will keep you from sinking too low and dissipating the forces generated that can be used in the following jump.

In a jump, the less you bend down and flex the legs and the faster you leave the ground, the higher you jump. This is due to energy accumulated from the forces withstood on landing and then given back in the take-off. This ability to accumulate energy and give it back quickly is the key to being able to jump very quickly, to gaining maximum height for multiple jumps and for extending distance if going three to five steps, as, for example, in the triple jump.

Strength Exercises

Improving the strength of the muscles involved can enhance jumping greatly. Strength exercises are also a prerequisite for doing explosive jump exercises. Some of the better exercises include:

Figure 6.1: Heel raise

1. Heel raises with Active Cords to improve ankle-joint extension and controlled flexion on touchdown (Figure 6.1).

2. Squats and deep jump squats for force in knee-joint extension.

3. The good morning for raising the trunk and strengthening the hamstrings.

4. Front arm raises from a back-lying position on a bench for more powerful arm action.

In addition, it is important to strengthen the lower-back muscles with exercises such as the back raise and back raise with a twist. Lower-back strength is very important in maintaining a rigid spine so that when the actual jump takes place there will be no cushioning in the mid-section to absorb the force generated by the legs. These exercises duplicate the motor pathways seen in the actual jump. Thus, they are of great benefit in improving jump height.

Other excellent exercises can be done not only for strengthening the joints involved but also for adding more force to the jump take-off. These include seated calf raises, leg extensions with the Active Cords, knee curls with the Active Cords, hip extension (pawback) with the Active Cords, glute-ham-gastroc raises, reverse trunk twist, lying front arm raises, shoulder shrugs and the overhead press.

Explosive Exercises

Increasing the strength of the muscles involved in jumping can show a significant improvement in jumping. However, for achieving maximum jump height, you must convert the strength to explosive power. Some of the better exercises that you can do include:

1. Double leg jumps in place.

2. Single leg jumps in place.

3. Double leg jumps with forward movement and with 90-180 degree turning for body control in space.

4. Single leg jumps with forward movement.

5. Depth jumps (shock method).

Each of these jumps should be the highest you can possibly go, and ground contact time should be minimized. In essence, as soon as you contact the ground, you absorb some of the initial forces for safety but then withstand most of the forces and return them as quickly as possible into the jump upward. When contact time is .15 seconds or less, you have a truly explosive jump. Also, do no more than 10 jumps in a row for one set. Doing more repetitions develops endurance rather than explosive power.

For more information on jumping and how it can be improved, see *Explosive Running*, *Explosive Basketball Training* and *Women's Soccer: Using Science to Improve Speed*.

NOTES:

Chapter 7
Throwing

Throwing appears to be a simple skill but, in fact, is a complex technique that requires many years of training in order to perform it well. The general body actions are learned in the early years, while in the teenage years the total skill is usually mastered. Perfection takes place in the ensuing years of competition or training.

It's not uncommon to hear people talk about throwing "like a girl" or having a "weak" or "strong" arm. However, comments such as these have little substance. Throwing technique or ability is not dif-

ferentiated by sex but determined mainly by what you learn and do in the early years. The saying, "throw like a girl," stems from the fact that in past years many girls, because of a lack of participation in sports and other activities, did very little throwing and never learned effective technique. They remained "body throwers," whereby the body and arm perform simultaneously. They did not have the ability to separate body and arm actions.

Figure 7.1: Front view of throw at release.

Cinematogram 7.1: Baseball Throw

Frame 1   Frame 2   Frame 3   Frame 4

Frame 5   Frame 6   Frame 7   Frame 8

Frame 9   Frame 10   Frame 11   Frame 12

Frame 13   Frame 14   Frame 15   Frame 16

Cinematogram 7.2: Baseball Throw with Preparatory Step

Frame 1 Frame 2 Frame 3 Frame 4 Frame 5 Frame 6

Frame 7 Frame 8 Frame 9 Frame 10 Frame 11

Frame 12 Frame 13 Frame 14 Frame 15 Frame 16

Frame 17 Frame 18 Frame 19 Frame 20 Frame 21 Frame 22

Cinematogram 7.3: Football Throw

Frame 1   Frame 2   Frame 3   Frame 4   Frame 5   Frame 6   Frame 7

Frame 8   Frame 9   Frame 10   Frame 11   Frame 12

Frame 13   Frame 14   Frame 15   Frame 16   Frame 17

Frame 18   Frame 19   Frame 20   Frame 21   Frame 22

Cinematogram 7.4: Ball Throw

Frame 1   Frame 2   Frame 3   Frame 4   Frame 5

Frame 6   Frame 7   Frame 8   Frame 9   Frame 10

Frame 11   Frame 12   Frame 13   Frame 14   Frame 15

Frame 16   Frame 17   Frame 18

People who throw this way are also usually weak throwers and often supinate (turn the palm of the hand toward you) the hand during the release. This leads to an even weaker throw. All strong or hard throwers pronate (turn the palm of the hand away from you during the release) the hand and have good separation and sequencing of body-joint actions to produce a maximum summation of force in the throw.

Because there is no universal teaching or sources of sound information on the basics of throwing, individuals learn mainly through trial and error. As a result, we see many different styles of throwing based on the person's physical characteristics and exposure to instruction. In general, it appears that the more sports a youngster participates in that involve throwing, the better his throwing becomes, mainly through trial and error and hopefully through some good instruction. The following is a brief description of throwing and some of the key factors that are involved.

Throwing begins with the legs (mainly the hip muscles), followed by the midsection (mainly the obliques), shoulder (rotator cuff) and then the muscles of the arm, wrist and hand. See Cinematograms 7.1, 7.2 and 7.3 for initial weight shift, stepping in toward the target and total throw. If the arm movements are learned first, developing the ability to use the body is more difficult, especially at a later age, because there is a tendency to rely more on arm power to generate force rather than the body. When the shoulder and arm muscles are the main sources of power, injuries usually occur to them. But when you master body movements (hips and midsection), execution of effective arm movements becomes relatively easy and safe.

To get the best use of your body and to create the most power, you must include weight shift and generate a summation of forces. Weight shift is a source of force production, but its main purpose is to help overcome inertia and to get the body and throwing implement in motion. Since the center of mass of the body is located in the hips, weight shift must include movement of the hips. Once the hips are in motion, the entire body is now in motion, ready to begin a powerful summation of forces. See Cinematograms 7.1, Frames 1-7; 7.2, Frames 6-12;

7.3, Frames 6-12 and 7.4, Frames 3-7 to see how the hips are shifted forward.

In summation of forces, there are sequential joint actions that follow a specific progression, culminating in maximum force in the hand at release. As your body weight is concluding its shift forward, the first action in the summation of forces is forward hip rotation. This action prepares the abdominal rotational muscles for the next action, which is shoulder girdle rotation. As the shoulder girdle rotation takes place, the arm is prepared for its medial rotation in the shoulder joint. This action prepares the wrist for wrist flexion, which then culminates in release of the ball. See Cinematograms 7.1, Frames 6-15; 7.2, Frames 12-17; 7.3, Frames 11-18 and 7.4, Frames 8-15.

If other body parts are included, such as the horizontal adduction of the arm after shoulder girdle rotation, it precedes the medial rotation. In other words, you can include other actions but they must fit in to the basic progression of body movements. You cannot go from the upper body to the lower body or vice versa and then back again, as this will break the sequence. There must be an orderly progression from the bottom (legs) working up to the top (hand) for ball release.

Stance

Throwing actions begin when in a side-facing position. You may start in a front-facing position as in the ready position, but you must then turn your body into a side-facing position before or as you begin the weight shift and forward stride. For example, see Cinematograms 7.1, Frames 1-5 and 7.3, Frames 1-5.

Weight Shift

The first action needed in throwing is weight shift, whereby the body and/or hips are moved forward to place weight on the forward leg. When shifting weight (moving body weight from the rear leg to the front leg), a short stride with the forward leg is taken after the muscles of the rear hip contract to push the pelvis forward (hip abduction). See Cinematograms 7.1, Frames 4-7 and 7.2, Frames 7-11.

Because you start with your weight on the rear leg, the front leg is free to move and comes forward as your hips are shifting forward.

See Cinematogram 7.3, Frames 6-11. Thus, when you step out during the weight shift, the muscles on both sides of the hips are in action. In the rear hip joint the abductor muscles contract to push the hips forward; in the front hip joint they contract to pull the leg out to take a step.

In some sports such as golf, only the hips can be in motion since the feet remain in place during the swing. Thus, to shift weight, only the hips are shifted forward. In a short, quick throw, when there is insufficient time to step forward, moving only the hips forward contributes to the production of force. The forward movement of the hips helps overcome inertia so that you can then execute sequential joint actions in the upper body to produce more force in the throw.

Summation of Forces

To produce as much force as possible, it is necessary to enlist the aid of as many joint actions and muscles as possible. When they occur in the correct sequence with the right timing, you maximize the amount of force produced in the release. In throwing, the following progression of body actions occurs during and after weight shift, which is a separate force added on to the total force produced.

First in the sequence of actions is forward hip rotation, which takes place as weight shift is ending and most of your weight is on the forward leg. See Cinematograms 7.1, Frames 6-9; 7.2, Frames 11-14; 7.3, Frames 12-14 and 7.4, Frames 7-10. The next action is shoulder rotation as the hip rotation is ending. Very often you see the shoulders and hips rotate at the same time because the athlete is unable to separate these movements. The key to more power is to get the hips started before the shoulders. This can be seen in Cinematograms 7.1, Frames 7-8; 7.2, Frames 12-13; 7.3, Frames 12-13 and 7.4, Frames 6-8.

When most of your weight is on your forward leg, hip rotation takes place around an axis through the front leg. This is advantageous for creating maximum force since the entire pelvic girdle rotates forward. If your weight remains equally balanced between both feet when you rotate the hips, the axis will be in the spine. In this case, the hip rotation produces very little force, mainly because you have equal

Cinematogram 7.5: Discus

Frame 1   Frame 2   Frame 3   Frame 4   Frame 5

Frame 6   Frame 7   Frame 8   Frame 9

Frame 10   Frame 11   Frame 12   Frame 13   Frame 14

Frame 15   Frame 16   Frame 17   Frame 18   Frame 19

weight of the hips moving backward as moving forward. This cancels the effects of each hip's rotation.

The hip rotation is a key action in throwing. It should occur as weight shift ends and before shoulder rotation begins. Keep these movements separate and combine them sequentially so that as one action ends the next action begins. For example, as weight shift is ending, the hips begin to accelerate. As the hips are decelerating, shoulder girdle rotation goes into acceleration. These actions can overlap one another and the ROM (range of motion) of each does not have to be great. The key is to exhibit them in the right sequence as in Cinematograms 7.1-7.4.

Cinematogram 7.6: Shot put

Frame 1   Frame 2   Frame 3   Frame 4   Frame 5

Frame 6   Frame 7   Frame 8   Frame 9   Frame 10

Frame 11   Frame 12   Frame 13   Frame 14   Frame 15   Frame 16

As the shoulder girdle rotation takes place, the arm is cocked — laterally rotated in the shoulder joint — which prepares the shoulder joint for action. After the lateral shoulder joint rotation, your body should be in an "arched bow" position, with the bow depicted by a reverse "C" curve of your backside. See Cinematograms 7.1, Frame 9; 7.2, Frame 14 and 7.4, Frame 10. In this position the abdominals are stretched and can contract more strongly to pull the upper body forward for even more force as the throw is executed. It is a consequence of effective body actions, not a separate action.

The arm then undergoes medial rotation after being laterally rotated in the cocking action, while the elbow remains bent at approximately 90 degrees or straightens somewhat. As the forward arm rotation takes place (shoulder-joint medial rotation), the upper arm remains in line with the shoulders while the forearm rotates forward. During this action, the wrist undergoes hyperextension in preparation for its action of flexion. See Cinematograms 7.1, Frames 9-12 and 7.4, Frames 10-11.

If elbow extension takes place, it changes the point of release to the side rather than close to the head. See Figure 7.1. If elbow extension is used to create more force in the throw, it can cause elbow and shoulder problems. This is often seen when players sling the ball out the side, a very common practice among some baseball pitchers.

Concentrate on keeping the elbow bent 90-120 degrees to create a whipping (recoil) action with the arm. As the forearm approaches the vertical (in the same plane as the shoulder) position, hand pronation (turning the hand toward the target) and wrist flexion (wrist flick) take place and the ball is released when the hand is in line with the ear and slightly in front. See Cinematograms 7.1, Frames 12-14 and 7.3, Frames 17-18.

Note that in Cinematogram 7.2, which was shot at a low shutter speed, all you can see is a blur for the arm action and the point where the ball release occurs. This indicates the speed with which the arm was moving when the release took place. You can see all of the body actions quite clearly, but the force generated by these actions as they move into the arm allow the arm to move at a very fast speed.

If you try to move the arm by itself, it would never come close to the speed generated with all of the prior body movements. This is how you can achieve 100 mile-per-hour throws. Also note the forward elbow position in Frames 12-13 in Cinematogram 7.4. This is a major fault and can lead to injury if the ball is thrown with great force, especially if emphasis is on elbow extension.

As the throwing pattern is mastered, it is important that you also practice throws from the opposite side. This is needed to produce more effective learning on the dominant side and to ensure proportional development of the body. In addition, the ability to throw right and left handed can be of great value in some sports.

Taking several steps before the throw enables you to get your total body moving forward. This creates considerable momentum so that when you plant the forward leg in the side-facing position, you must block it strongly and then go through the motions as outlined above. See Cinematogram 7.2, Frames 1-11. In this way, you get additional force from the initial momentum developed, which is then transferred into the summation of forces, culminating in a longer and/or more powerful throw than if you did not have an approach.

At times, you may also see an athlete take a skip before planting the final leg or combining it with a few steps and then getting set to throw. It doesn't make much difference which pattern you use since the forward movement and body positioning are the key elements.

Underhand and side-arm throws involve the same body actions but with some changes in the arm action. For example, in the underhand throw, as in fast-pitch softball, there is weight shift during the powerful forward stride (skip), followed by hip rotation then followed by shoulder rotation as the arm goes through a windmill pattern to release the ball alongside the hip.

The side-arm pattern, which requires modified body actions, depends on the exact positioning of the hand with the ball. For example, if the ball is below the waist it is difficult to rotate the hips first. Thus, the throw relies mainly on shoulder rotation and arm actions. If the throw is between the hips and shoulders, then the hips can come through first, followed by the arm in a sideward pattern.

In the discus throw, because of the limited area allowed, athletes combine rotational and linear movements to create additional force rather than only forward linear movements as when throwing a baseball or javelin. However, the basic body actions are still the same. In the shoulder joint, there is a greater horizontal adduction, while in the wrist joint, there is ulna flexion rather than flexion. See Cinematogram 7.5.

In the shot-put, because of the heavier implement being used, there is exhibited a combination of the throwing sequence actions and a pushing pattern. In other words, there is greater overlap between the hip, shoulder and arm movements. The heavier implement does not allow you to execute all the movements as described in the throwing pattern above. See Cinematogram 7.6. Thus, we see that for every implement being used and every amount of weight, there are adaptations that must be made to accommodate the extra resistance or the object of the throw.

The following are some of the better strength exercises that you can use to help you not only master but perfect the throw, regardless of the implement or the resistance you are using.

1. Hip abduction (forward stride), resistance from rubber tubing and a hip belt as in the Active Cords set (Figure 7.2).

2. Hip rotation with and without resistance from the Active Cords.

3. Side lunge with and without resistance from the Active Cords.

4. Reverse trunk twist to improve midsection flexibility and strength of the abdominal rotational muscles.

5. T-bench medial rotation to strengthen the shoulder (arm) medial rotators as they are used in throwing (Figure 7.3).

Figure 7.2: Weight shift and hip turn

Frame 1

Frame 2

Figure 7.3: T-bench medial rotation

Frame 1   *Frame 2*   *Frame 3*

Figure 7.4: Medicine ball throw

Frame 1   *Frame 2*   *Frame 3*

6. Lateral shoulder rotation with a dumbbell while in a prone position.

7. Lateral prone raise to help prevent rotator cuff injury which typically occurs in the follow-through on the back of the shoulders.

8. Triceps push-down with the palm-up and palm-down grips for elbow stabilization and strength.

9. Supination/pronation with the strength bar to develop the rotational ability of the forearm and prevent tennis elbow.

10. Wrist curls for the wrist-flick action.

11. Catching and throwing medicine balls to develop explosive midsection rotational power (Figure 7.4).

12. Catching and throwing dropped balls while in a supine position with medial shoulder rotation with and without the wrist flick.

Chapter 8
Hitting/Striking

The stance and major body actions in hitting are similar to throwing. In the initial stance when hitting a baseball, softball, hand ball, golf or tennis ball, you assume a side-facing position. You may start in a front-facing position as in the ready position in tennis and handball, but you turn into the side-facing position when preparing to hit.

The first action in preparing to hit is performed as you turn to face sideways (or when already facing sideways): a weight shift via hip abduction. In this you shift the hips forward so that your weight moves onto the front leg. See Cinematogram 8.1, Frames 1-4; 8.2, Frames 2-4; 8.3, Frames 1-6 and 8.4, Frames 4-8.

As the weight shift onto the front leg is occuring or concluding, hip rotation takes place. See Cinematograms 8.3, Frames 8-10 and 8.4, Frames 7-10.) If you have a strong weight shift, as when hitting for maximum power, the axis should be in the forward hip joint and leg. An exception to this is when baseball players forcefully straighten the forward leg to push the hips into backward rotation and pivot on the rear foot and leg, known as the sit-and-pivot swing. See Cinematogram 8.2, Frames 5-7 and 8.3, Frames 4-6. This creates faster body rotation but not always more hits. For this reason, this technique is not recommended for youngsters who are first mastering their

Cinematogram 8.1: Underhand hit

Frame 1   Frame 2   Frame 3   Frame 4

Frame 5   Frame 6   Frame 7   Frame 8

hitting technique. They should be concerned with getting more hits, not home runs.

If you shift your weight forward until there is an equal balance between the legs or there is slightly more weight on the forward leg, there will be less force in the hip rotation. But you will still be able to generate great force.

As the hips rotate forward, the shoulders should remain in a side-facing position. This is needed so the abdominal rotational muscles that pull the shoulder girdle around in the next action are stretched for a stronger contraction. See Cinematogram 8.1, Frames 3-5. Most players, however, rotate the shoulders together with the hips. This produces a loss in power. This is especially evident in Cinematogram 8.2, Frames 4-6 and Cinematogram 8.4, Frames 8-10.

At the same time, the arm(s) holding the hitting implement should be brought back further to the rear to stretch the shoulder muscles even more and to create greater force during the forward swing. However, when time is of the essence, this becomes impossible, as it takes more time to execute the swing. This is especially true in baseball and

Cinematogram 8.2: Baseball swing

Frame 1   Frame 2   Frame 3   Frame 4   Frame 5

Frame 6   Frame 7   Frame 8   Frame 9   Frame 10

tennis when, as the hip rotation is ending, shoulder rotation begins via strong contraction of the abdominal oblique muscles. When there is limited time, the amount of hip rotation is small. Thus the key to creating the greatest power is to have the hips rotate before the shoulders. The quicker and faster this is done, the more power you can generate.

As the shoulder girdle rotates forward, the upper body ends up in a front-facing position when contact occurs. See Cinematograms 8.1, Frames 4-6; 8.2, Frames 6-7 and 8.3, Frames 8-9, 8.4, Frames 11-12 and 8.5, frame 3. When you cannot use the hips effectively, as in a low hit in a side-facing position, shoulder rotation plays the major role in force production. See Cinematograms 8.1 and 8.5. Sometimes it is possible to see an arched bow posture, similar to throwing during contact.

Because the arms are connected to the shoulders, as the forward shoulder rotation is taking place the arm(s) are also in motion. Thus, in addition to generating up to 30 percent of the total force, the shoulder rotation also plays a major role in the initial acceleration of the arm(s) prior to their independent arm action. When the shoulder joint

Cinematogram 8.3: Baseball swing

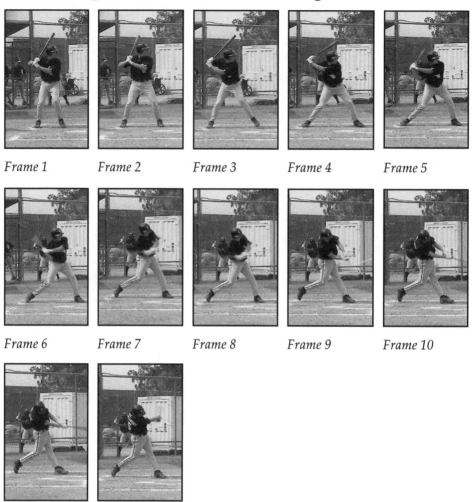

Frame 1   Frame 2   Frame 3   Frame 4   Frame 5

Frame 6   Frame 7   Frame 8   Frame 9   Frame 10

Frame 11   Frame 12

muscles contract to move the arm(s), they impart even more speed (force) to the hitting implement.

In the baseball hit, the arms extend forward as the shoulders face front (Cinematograms 8.2, Frames 7-10 and 8.3, Frames 6-10), while in the tennis forehand the arm travels with the shoulders and then moves forward independently to make contact (Cinematogram 8.4, Frames 10-13). In the golf swing, the shoulders bring the arms around and then the arms act independently through contact (Cinematogram 8.6, Frames 8-11). In handball, once the shoulders have rotated for-

Cinematogram 8.4: Tennis Forehand

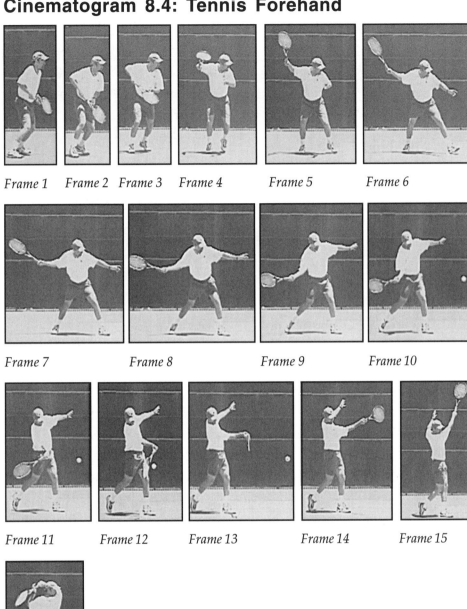

Frame 1   Frame 2   Frame 3   Frame 4   Frame 5   Frame 6

Frame 7   Frame 8   Frame 9   Frame 10

Frame 11   Frame 12   Frame 13   Frame 14   Frame 15

Frame 16

Cinematogram 8.5: Fly hit (sidearm)

Frame 1   *Frame 2*   *Frame 3*   *Frame 4*   *Frame 5*

Frame 6

ward, the arm takes over (Cinematogram 8.1, Frames 4-7 and Cinematogram 8.5, Frames 2-5).

In most hitting actions there are also strong wrist actions to accelerate the hitting implement even more or to help maintain speed. For example, in golf and baseball swings, the wrists undergo ulna flexion (the little-finger side of the hands moves toward the forearm) while the arms are relatively stationary to create more speed at the end of the hitting implement. This action is needed to bring the lagging hitting implement square to the ball for greater distance (power) and accuracy. The wrist action then stops momentarily as the hitting implement continues moving forward while remaining perpendicular (square) to the ball. It picks up again in the follow-through. See Cinematogram 8.2, Frames 8-10; 8.3, Frames 6-10 and 8.6, Frames 8-12.

In the tennis forehand, the wrists undergo slight hyperextension just before and after the contact phase so that the racquet moves in a straight line for maximum hitting accuracy. See Cinematogram 8.4,

Cinematogram 8.6: Golf swing

Frame 1   Frame 2   Frame 3   Frame 4

Frame 5   Frame 6   Frame 7   Frame 8

Frame 9   Frame 10   Frame 11   Frame 12

Frame 13   Frame 14

Frames 10-13. In the handball fly hit you can see the wrist cock (hyperextend) and then flex to make contact. Pronation also takes place to add spin to the ball. See Cinematogram 8.5, Frames 2-4.

In the swing you strive to move the hitting implement in a straight line, perpendicular to the intended flight line during the contact phase. This is why the wrist stays firm during contact. In addition, the grip is tight so as not to allow any movement. In general, the more wrist action you use to bring the hitting implement around prior to contact, the more power you can generate. Some players, however, use very little wrist action and rely more on shoulder rotation to bring the hitting implement into contact with the ball.

It is possible to find many variations in hitting that depend on your abilities and how much time is available to execute the swing. For example, when batting against a fastball pitcher in baseball, you have about .25 seconds to execute the swing. Because of this, the amount of hip rotation is reduced, and you rely more on shoulder rotation to bring around the bat. However, with strength and explosive training, execution time can be decreased so that additional body parts can be involved for more power. In addition, the swing can occur later, giving you more time to read the pitch. Vision training is also beneficial for seeing and contacting the ball.

In the ideal hit, the center of gravity of the object being hit should be aligned with the center of gravity of the hitting implement. In this case there are no vibrational forces created on contact. When the hit is off center there is a tendency for the hitting implement to rotate, which creates stress in the forearm and elbow if your grip is not sufficiently strong. During contact the grip should be tight so that all the forces generated by the body and arm(s) can be transferred to the hitting implement. A relaxed grip absorbs the forces, resulting in a weaker hit. However, a relaxed grip in the initial stance or the beginning of the swing is desirable. As the swing proceeds, the grip should tighten and be very tight on impact.

Figure 8.1: Finger flexion with ExerRing

Strength Exercises

Many of the same strength exercises used in throwing are used to improve hitting. The most important exercises are hip abduction, side lunge with the Active Cords, medial and lateral rotation in the hip joints (hip rotation), back raises, back raises with a twist, reverse trunk twist, Russian twist, lateral prone raises (reverse flyes), tricep push-downs and/or narrow grip bench press, supination-pronation and ulna-radial flexion with the strength bar, wrist curls and reverse curls, and finger flexion and grip with ExerRings (Figure 8.1).

Figure 8.1, Frame 2

NOTES:

Chapter 9
Kicking

The mechanics of kicking are the same for all sports and for all types of balls kicked, including footballs, soccer balls or rugby balls. The major differences between kicks relate to the angle of approach to the ball and whether the ball is resting on the ground, supported on a tee or moving through space.

All players execute the same joint actions when kicking, but the range of motion, the force and speed of movement of the limbs, body posture and timing of the actions can be quite different, resulting in different-looking kicks. This is obvious when you look at the cinematograms presented in this chapter. Each kick looks different from the others, yet they all involve the same actions. The kick can also look somewhat different depending on where the point of contact is made on the foot, which in turn produces a different effect.

Technique

Although kicking occurs with the leg, hip and shoulder rotation also play important roles. The need for and importance of these joint actions increase greatly when kicking for distance and/or producing more force. For example, when approaching the ball from a position 10-30 degrees to the side (see Cinematograms 9.1, 9.2 and 9.3) and straight on (Cinematogram 9.4), as the support foot is planted and

Cinematogram 9.1: Soccer kick, side view

Frame 1   Frame 2   Frame 3   Frame 4

Frame 5   Frame 6   Frame 7   Frame 8

Frame 9   Frame 10   Frame 11   Frame 12

Frame 13   Frame 14   Frame 15   Frame 16

your body weight is supported by the front leg, the kicking leg is behind the body with the hips rotated to the rear.

This action stretches the hip rotational and hip-flexor muscles of the kicking leg, which produces stronger muscular contractions when bringing the hips and thigh forward for the kick. See Cinematograms 9.1, Frame 4; 9.2, Frame 2 and 9.3, Frames 3-4.

As the forward leg is placed in support alongside the middle or middle-back portion of the ball, the kick is initiated. The hips (pelvic girdle) rotate forward to bring the kicking leg directly behind the ball in line with the target, and to initiate forward movement of the thigh. The main action begins as the hips are ending their forward rotation. See Cinematograms 9.1, Frames 4-8; 9.2, Frames 3-5 and 9.3, Frames 4-6.

As the thigh moves forward, there is additional knee bending to stretch the quadriceps muscle of the anterior thigh. See Cinematograms 9.1, Frames 3-7 and 9.2, Frames 2-5. This prepares the muscles for

Cinematogram 9.2: Soccer kick

Frame 1

Frame 2   *Frame 3*   *Frame 4*   *Frame 5*

Frame 6   *Frame 7*   *Frame 8*   *Frame 9*

Cinematogram 9.3: Soccer kick, side view

Frame 1   Frame 2   Frame 3   Frame 4

Frame 5   Frame 6   Frame 7   Frame 8

Frame 9   Frame 10   Frame 11   Frame 12

Frame 13   Frame 14   Frame 15   Frame 16

Cinematogram 9.4: Soccer kick, front view

Frame 1 Frame 2 Frame 3 Frame 4

Frame 5 Frame 6 Frame 7 Frame 8

Frame 9 Frame 10 Frame 11 Frame 12

Frame 13 Frame 14 Frame 15 Frame 16

the knee extension action which follows. See Cinematograms 9.1, Frames 8-12; 9.2, Frames 5-8 and 9.3, Frames 5-8.

The thigh is driven forward until it is 20-30 degrees in front of the body, although some knee extension begins prior to this point as the thigh slows down and momentarily stops. As the leg extends, the shin is whipped forward vigorously to contact the ball with the foot, and the leg becomes fully extended. The ball should leave the foot at this point. Notice how on each of the kickers the leg is still slightly bent at the knee when the ball leaves the foot. A nearly straight leg is seen on the kicker in Cinematogram 9.1 who was an All-American collegiate player. The straight leg then goes into the follow-through as the ball leaves the foot. See Cinematograms 9.1, Frames 8-13; 9.2, Frames 5-8 and 9.3, Frames 5-8.

Cinematograms 9.2 and 9.3 show the kick of successful soccer players. However, rather than staying over the ball as the former All-American player does in Cinematogram 9.1, they do not move

Cinematogram 9.5: Soccer kick

Frame 1

Frame 2　　　　*Frame 3*　　　　*Frame 4*　　　　*Frame 5*

Frame 6　　　　*Frame 7*　　　　*Frame 8*　　　　*Frame 9*

the upper body weight forward. This reduces the power generated. The player in Cinematogram 9.2 raises the thigh too high, forcing him to contact the ball with the toe of the foot resulting in a low trajectory.

In order to keep the ball moving in a straight line toward the target, the shoulders rotate in the opposite direction from the hips to counterbalance their movement. For example, for a right-legged kicker there is a tendency for the hips to continue rotating to the left. To counteract this action the shoulders rotate to the right to hold the hips square to the target and to allow the leg to swing through on a straight line toward the target. See Cinematograms 9.1, Frames 9-14 and 9.2, Frames 6-8. Note that the shoulders (and arms) begin the counter rotation soon after the support leg is planted, with most of the action occurring during and after the contact phase.

Guidelines to Improve Kicking Skills and Prevent Injury

Making contact with the ball on the inside of the foot along the long edge of the shoe and inside ankle bone is mainly used for passing. It is not considered a strong kicking action. The large surface area created by the foot in this position provides greater control and makes it easier to direct the ball to a specific spot. In contrast, kicking the ball with the toe of the shoe uses a very small surface area (Cinematogram 9.2). Because of this the kick is often erratic and as a result, this contact point is seldom used.

When kicking for distance or force, it is most effective to make contact above the instep of the foot. This means that the ball should make contact on the laces of the shoe or the area slightly below and/ or above the laces. To create such contact the player should point the toe downward and slightly inward when kicking. See Cinematogram 9.1, Frames 10-12; 9.3, Frame 7 and 9.5, Frames 5-6.

At times, it is necessary to lean to the outside away from the support leg to give greater clearance for the kicking leg coming through and to provide a different point of contact. Maintaining this position requires additional balance and physical strength. If you do not have the ability to do this, you could risk injuring your foot if it makes contact with the ground prior to the ball.

As a player masters the basic skill of kicking, variations should be introduced, such as approaching the ball from different angles and with different speed run-ups, kicking a bouncing ball, kicking a ball in flight and so on. For each of these variants, adjustments must be made in body position, balance and kicking actions.

Strength and Flexibility Exercises

To enhance learning and mastery of the kick, it is necessary to strengthen the muscles as they are used in kicking. Note that the actions and muscles involved are the same as in running! As a result of strength training, you can increase the range of motion and apply more force and accuracy to the ball. For example, in order to maintain stability on the support leg, do supplementary eccentric and isometric training of the leg muscles. The best exercises are squats and delay squats.

To develop the hip flexibility and strength of the hip flexor muscles, you should do hip rotation and the classic lunge exercise with dumbbells and/or with Active Cords. Be sure to take a long step to ensure an adequate stretch of the hip flexors of the rear leg. To make the exercise more specific, do the lunge with a powerful forward drive using the Active Cords and work up to a leap in the lunge. Hold the bottom position for a couple of seconds.

For the midsection, the reverse trunk twist is a good exercise for rotating the shoulders forward, and the back raise with a twist is beneficial for rotating the shoulders backward. The use of these muscles depends on your posture during and after contact. Use Active Cords to work on knee extension with the thigh raised and in front of the body (Figure 9.1). To enhance hip rotation do hip rotation exercises using Active Cords, rotating the hips forcefully with and against the resistance of the Cords.

Figure 9.1: Leg (knee) extension with active cords

Chapter 10
Strength Training

Strength, the ability to create and/or maintain force, is perhaps the most important physical quality for success in sports. The main reason for this is that strength is related to many other physical and mental qualities. For example:

1) Strength is needed to assume and maintain static and dynamic posture. In the execution of sports skills, as the body changes position the muscles must constantly make corrections to maintain the body in a safe and effective position.

2) Strength holds the spine (often rigid) in its normal, safe curvature. This is important when executing strength exercises and sports skills and when transferring force from the legs to the upper body and vice versa.

3) Strength is needed to demonstrate active flexibility.

Athletes often use static stretching during which you hold a position for 30-60 seconds. Such stretching does not prevent injury nor does it prepare the muscles for action, the main purpose of stretching in a warm-up. Muscle strength moves the body and limbs through the needed range of motion (flexibility) and provides the force for these movements. Prolonged static stretching overstretches ligaments and tendons, making you more prone to injury.

4) Greater strength produces greater speed and force. In general, the more strength you have, the greater the force that you can exhibit in running, kicking, throwing, hitting, etc. When coupled with speed (speed-strength), it is the key to quick, fast and explosive movements.

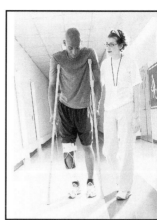

Figure 10.1: Rehabilitation

5) Greater strength gives you better control of your body movements — neuromuscular coordination — the key element in the execution of all sports skills. The strength enables your movements to be executed safely and effectively.

6) With greater strength, you develop a better muscular feel of the various joint actions. This is needed to perfect your sports technique. Strength allows you to practice a particular movement correctly to develop neuromuscular (motor) pathways that will feel natural.

7) You need strength to learn a skill (technique). Strength allows you to execute your sports skills effectively and to learn key actions to improve your skill. This is especially evident when first attempting new or different movements. If you do not have the strength to carry out new actions, you develop poor or even potentially dangerous skill patterns that may be extremely difficult to change after solidified. As a result, you will be limited when trying to improve your performance.

8) Strength helps to prevent injury. Effective technique, adequate flexibility, muscle strength and strong tendons and ligaments help prevent injury. If your joints are well stabilized and under the control of the muscles when

Figure 10.2: Breathing after a run

forces are encountered, the chances of injury are minimal. Also, since all skills are under neuromuscular control, any dysfunction may create injury in addition to lack of strength.

Figure 10.3: Swimming

9) Strength speeds up rehabilitation. If you happen to get injured but have adequate strength levels, you will recover faster. Strength training is one of the primary methods used in rehabilitation of injuries.

10) Strength improves breathing abilities. Breathing plays an important role in the execution of almost all skills and in relaxation. When your respiratory muscles are strong, you are capable of taking in and processing more air per breath to get greater amounts of oxygen for energy production, preventing the onset of fatigue and helping in recovery.

11) Greater strength can improve your aerobic capabilities. When you engage in aerobic conditioning, your cardiovascular and respiratory functions improve, but strength does not. By developing greater muscle strength, you will be able to do aerobic activities more effectively and experience greater gains.

12) Strength (and other physical qualities) develops greater confidence, the most important psychological quality you must possess in order to be successful. Confidence is based on your ability to execute skills when necessary. It is the key to consistent and well-executed play.

13) Greater strength develops greater mental abilities. Science has shown that only about 10 percent of human brain cells participate in mental activities. What has been overlooked is that the remaining 90 percent of the brain participates directly in the function of different organs, including the muscles, during the

mental activity. If you deprive the brain of impulses from these organs, you would plunge into a deep sleep.

Thus, signals from the muscles are a necessary prerequisite for successful brain activity. Strength training is best for maximum nervous pulsation in a minimum amount of time to quickly remove psycho-emotional tension and mental fatigue and improve mental abilities.

As you become stronger and more fit, you learn what it takes to overcome difficulties in life. For example, I once had a student who was required to swim one mile using any stroke or combination of strokes without stopping or holding onto the sides of the pool. She had to be in motion at all times but could float when she felt tired. Of all the girls in the class, she was the least coordinated and had participated minimally in physical activities during her elementary and high school years. To pass the class, she practiced almost every day.

By the end of the semester, she successfully finished the mile swim. A few days later she told me that my class did more to change her life than any other experience. She now realized she could accomplish anything she wanted to, both physically and mentally. In her words, this was a turning point in her life. It made her realize that she was capable of much more than she had ever dreamed possible.

The same thing can happen to you. In order to succeed in your sport, you will find that training at times is serious, difficult, sometimes miserable work, and not fun and games. As a result, you develop perseverance, tenacity, at times aggressiveness and other psychological qualities to do the work that is needed to succeed. The more you practice, the more accomplished you will become and the greater the effect will be on your mind and body.

14) You need strength for relaxation. When you are under tension, the muscles are in a state of contraction. Thus, before you can relax the tension must be removed. If not, relaxation is impossible. By contracting the muscles during exertion, the muscles

relax on the return phase. If not, you must consciously think of relaxation on the return. You must also learn to relax muscles that are not involved in the exercise. This conserves energy, keeps you relaxed and thinking more clearly so that you can better adapt to changing situations during game play.

The Different Forms of Strength

There are three major types of strength that must be differentiated for training purposes. Each plays a different role in training and in specific sports.

1) **Concentric strength**, in which the muscle shortens during the contraction, is known as an overcoming-type contraction. You overcome a resistance by moving it through a particular range of motion (ROM).

2) **Eccentric strength**, in which the muscle lengthens (returns to its original length) during its contraction, is known as a yielding and stopping type of contraction.The muscle yields to the outside force and stops a movement.

3) **Isometric strength**, in which there is some shortening of the muscle fibers but no joint movement, is known as a static or holding contraction.

Figure 10.4, Frame 1

All movements require these three muscle contraction regimes. For example, when doing a biceps-curl exercise, the biceps and other elbow flexor muscles shorten (concentric contraction) to bring the forearm and weight upward. When the weight is lowered the muscles are still under tension to control the downward movement against the force of gravity, the force pulling the weight downward. The muscles lengthen (yield to gravity) as they resist the downward force while under eccentric contraction. When

Figure 10.4, Frame 2

the eccentric contraction becomes strong enough it stops the downward movement at any point and the muscle contraction switches to isometric as you hold the position. When you return to the bottom position the muscles relax but still maintain some tension to take stress off the elbow and possibly shoulder joints (Figure 10.4).

The eccentric contraction, which is 50 percent stronger than the concentric, is a key to success in explosive (speed-strength) movements. It is used in all stopping actions when running, catching a ball or repelling an opponent, and prepares a muscle for an explosive contraction by pre-tensing it. The stronger the eccentric contraction the sooner you can stop a movement and switch the contraction to concentric, putting you in action. The greater the tension in the eccentric contraction, the quicker the stop and change in direction.

In the isometric contraction, the muscle can undergo up to 20 percent greater force than in the concentric. The muscular force is great enough to hold a position and to pre-tense a muscle, preparing it for action.

When discussing strength it is also necessary to distinguish between the various ways it is trained and displayed. For example, **absolute strength** is the maximum strength you can exhibit in the concentric, eccentric or isometric regime. Most often it is measured in the concentric regime. Absolute strength has a unique relationship to speed and explosiveness. For a youngster or novice athlete, increasing the absolute levels of strength has a direct positive effect on the execution of the sports skills and on speed and explosiveness.

Once you have achieved high levels of absolute strength, further increases in strength lead to a decrease in speed and explosiveness, which is especially visible in high-level athletes. It is a catch-22 situation: on the one hand you want to increase absolute strength to improve performance, but on the other hand you do not want more strength at the expense of speed and explosiveness. The bottom line is that you should never increase strength to such a level that it leads to a slow down in the execution of the sports skill, speed or explosiveness.

When you are a well-trained athlete you should do speed and explosive training after every significant increase in absolute strength.

Understand that when you do explosive or plyometric-type movements, you only use about 80 percent of your total absolute strength. To become more explosive, you must increase your absolute strength levels and then literally convert the newly developed strength to greater speed and explosiveness.

Figure 10.5: Basketball

Explosive strength relates to how quickly and forcefully the muscles contract, the key to all quick movements. To elicit explosive strength, the muscles and tendons must be pre-tensed eccentrically before contracting. When the tension is sufficiently great, the muscular contraction switches to concentric — the muscle and tendon shorten very quickly to start the movement and explosive strength is then displayed.

Speed-strength is synonymous with explosiveness or explosive power and is exhibited in movements that require speed coupled with strength. Speed of movement is the key component for success in sports that require quick execution of the skills. The faster and more forcefully the skills are executed, the more successful you usually are.

Starting strength is the ability to move quickly out of a stationary position. This requires effective technique, good reaction time and the ability to stimulate the muscles as quickly as possible to get them into action with great speed. Reaction time for the most part is innate, but your ability to get the muscles into action with speed and power can be improved. Using explosive isometrics and other forms of true plyometric training will train your muscles to figuratively explode and quickly move you out of a stationary position. Technique is very important in starting strength.

Figure 10.6: The start

Functional strength is a popular term in the sports world but has different meanings. In general, your strength is functional only if it is exhibited in your skill execution. For example, if a basketball player can squat with 400 pounds and has a vertical jump of two

Figure 10.7: Middle-distance runner

feet his strength is not as functional as a basketball player who can squat 300 pounds but has a three-foot vertical jump.

The athlete who can jump the highest has the potential to become the more successful athlete, regardless of the fact that he may not squat with as much weight as others. The key is to develop strength that can be incorporated into your sports skill so that it improves a specific aspect of your performance. Specificity of strength is a more accurate term than functional strength.

Strength-endurance applies to how many repetitions you can do of a strength exercise, as for example, completing 25 or more repetitions of the bench press. It can also apply to repeating skills requiring an element of strength, such as repeating the same stride in a mid-distance race. The key to success is to continually exhibit the same technique and not have it change because of decreasing strength.

General vs. Specialized Strength Exercises

An exercise does not have the same effect nor does it improve sports performance to the same degree for athletes at different levels of development. The impact of an exercise also depends on whether it has a direct effect on your sports skill. For example:

General Strength Exercises are those exercises that are used in overall body conditioning. They are not directly related to the specific actions seen in the sports skill. The overhead press exercise for runners can be used to illustrate this concept. It is a common exercise in which the arms move sideways directly upward from the shoulders. In running, however, the arms move in a forward-backward motion in relation to the trunk. Thus, while the overhead press is a good exercise for strengthening the shoulders and arms, which are used in running, it does not duplicate the arm and shoulder movements in the exact actions (pathways) used in running, and so does little to improve your sports skill. But general exercises serve as a base upon which you can add specialized exercises.

When the movement pattern in the exercise duplicates what occurs in the run (or sports skill), it is known as a specialized exercise. For a runner, an example of a specialized exercise for the shoulders and arms is driving your arm from behind your body to the front of your body in the same pathway and in the same range of motion as in the running stride.

Specialized Strength Exercises are designed and selected so that the movements and actions closely match those seen in the execution of the sports skill. They also promote psychological traits such as decisiveness, willpower, perseverance and confidence to achieve specific goals. They have similar concentration and psychological qualities as those seen in competition.

For example, execution of certain specialized exercises requires concentration to develop the neuromuscular pathway needed. A strength exercise that duplicates one aspect of a skill requires ultimate concentration and perseverance to repeat exactly the same movement time after time to develop the necessary muscle feel. For the specialized exercises to have maximum positive transfer you must be decisive in your movements and actions to develop the confidence to repeat the action during play.

Criteria for Specialized Strength Exercises

1. The exercise must duplicate the exact movement witnessed in certain actions of the sports skill. One example would be an exercise to duplicate the exact ankle, knee, hip or shoulder joint action.

2. The exercise must involve the same type of muscular contraction as used in execution of the skill. For example, in the push-off in sprinting, the calf muscles undergo an explosive shortening contraction (after being

Figure 10.8: Explosive lunge to duplicate the push-off

pre-tensed in the landing) to produce maximum force. Thus the special exercise must also include an explosive muscular contraction as occurs in the calf muscle (Figure 10.8).

Figure 10.9: Golfer

3. In a specialized exercise you develop strength and flexibility in the same range of motion (ROM) as in the actual skill. For example, pitchers and golfers need powerful rotational strength when starting shoulder rotation in the forward swing. This occurs after the shoulders are rotated to the rear, not from a front- facing position. Specialized exercises that develop strength in this ROM include the reverse trunk twist and Russian twist. Exercises such as the crunch with a twist or sit-up with a twist do not duplicate the ROM and thus are considered general exercises.

The concept of exercise specificity is new to sports but the term "specificity" is not. Many authors use the term "specific exercises" but few exercises actually fulfill the above criteria. Theses authors use the term when referring to exercises that strengthen the muscles used in a skill, but do not match the particular way they are used in the skill. Thus they are general exercises and are still of value in the general physical preparation period.

Typical strength and conditioning programs for athletes include general exercises to get them in shape. The prescribed exercises may use the same muscles as used in the sport skill, but if these exercises do not fulfill the above criteria, they will not directly improve your skill.

Breathing

When you perform strength exercises, your breathing technique is very important. Because of this, you should develop proper breathing patterns from the start. For example, to do a strength exercise correctly you should inhale and hold your breath on the exertion—that is, on the hardest part of the exercise, when you are overcoming resistance. You exhale on the return, staying in control of the movements. This is the oppostie of what you often hear or read from other sources — that you should exhale on the exertion and inhale on the return.

The widely used recommendation to exhale on exertion is based on theory, not research or practice, and applies mainly

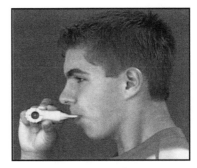

Figure 10.10: Breathing against resistance

to people with heart and circulatory system problems. If you are without cardiovascular problems (as you should be if you are an athlete) and do not hold your breath for more than a few seconds as needed in maximum weight strength exercises, breath-holding on exertion is perfectly safe. It makes the exercise safer and more effective.

Inhaling and holding your breath on exertion comes naturally. Many studies have shown that when you execute a skill, you hold your breath on the exertion—during the power phase, when force is generated. The breath-holding on exertion provides up to 20 percent greater force, stabilizes the spine, and helps prevent lower back injuries. It transforms the trunk (and, in fact, the whole body) into a stable unit against which your hips, shoulders and arms can move more effectively.

Breathing exercises can also help you relax. For example, inhaling then exhaling before starting in a race or shooting a basket is a good technique to help you relax. But before starting, it is important that the muscles have some tension—not excessive tension, but sufficient tension to produce power. Do not take a maximal breath and then hold it, as this can make you uncomfortable. Take a breath slightly greater than usual and then hold it to experience the positive benefits.

Developing Strength

Strength appears to be the simplest, but is in fact the most complex physical quality to be developed. The type of equipment and exercises you use, how you perform the exercises, and the training regime all play very important roles in determining your results .

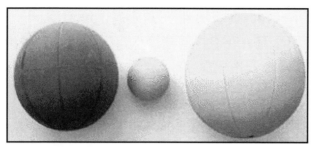
Figure 10.11: Medicine balls

Free weights are recommended over machine weights for almost all athletes. The reason for this is that when you use free weights (barbells, dumbbells, medicine balls, rubber tubing, etc.), you can move the resistance in a manner more suited to the sports skill's neuromuscular pattern. With free weights, you must guide and control the movement throughout the execution. In the process you develop balance and stability because the total body participates in every exercise, especially when relatively heavy weights are used.

When you use machine weights you must do what the machine dictates. You are guided by the machine rather than by what the body or limbs are intended to do. For this reason, machine exercises are useful for general conditioning purposes, not specificity.

Medicine balls are used in many different exercises to develop strength, but their greatest value lies in explosive midsection and arm training. The sudden forces experienced upon catching a weighted ball also imitates what happens in contact sports when you make contact with another player.

Active Cords (special rubber tubing with attachments) allow you to duplicate movement patterns seen in the execution of sports skills that cannot be done with dumbbells, barbells or exercise machines. With the Active Cords, you can create resistance in any and all directions so that replication of the sports skill movement pattern is possible.

The rubber tubing must have specific tensions and accessories so it can be attached to different parts of the body, as well as to different objects on the field, in the gym or at home. With these criteria in mind, I created the Active Cords set, which consists of three different tension tubes with metal swivel clasps, each of which can be used independently or collectively to provide the greatest resistance (see Figure 10.12). There are also two handles to which the tubing can be attached for arm and shoulder work; a non-slip belt that goes around the hips for rotational, lunging and leaping exercises; and an ankle- and dual-attachment strap that can be used in a doorway or around a stationary beam, post or fence.

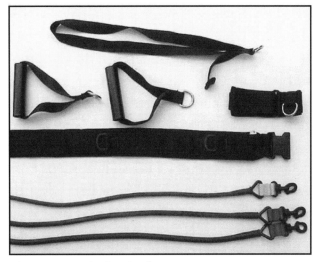

Figure 10.12: Active Cords set

For more information on this equipment and related exercises, see the books listed at the end of this chapter or contact: Sports Training Inc., P. O. Box 460429, Escondido, CA 92046. Telephone, (760) 480-0558 or visit www.DrYessis.com.

Weight, Sets and Reps

Most athletes want to know how much weight they should use and how many sets and reps they should perform for each exercise. However, understand that there is no single best amount of weight or best number of sets and reps. The exact figures depend upon many factors, but most importantly include your stage of training, your level of fitness and the purpose of the exercise. The number of sets and reps and the amount of weight used will bring about different results at different stages of training and levels of performance. Also, the weight you use is determined by the type of strength you are trying to increase.

When first beginning strength training, the number of sets should be low, as the results you attain will be the same regardless of how many sets you do. In general, starting with 15-20 repetitions maximum (RM) is best when first developing a strength and muscular endurance base. You incorporate changes after the base training to make the number of sets and reps more specific to your objectives.

The length of time that you stay with any one routine is determined by your level of ability and type of training being done. For example, if you are a beginner developing a general strength base, you may stay with the same program for several months. If you are a high-level athlete in the general conditioning phase, you may stay with general training for two to four weeks before advancing to more specialized work. Thus, all aspects of the weight training program are determined by your stage in the annual training cycle as well as your age, level of fitness, exercise mastery, objectives and so on.

The amount of weight that you use determines, to a large extent, the amount of strength, mass, endurance or speed that you can gain. For example, using close to maximum weight so that you can only do one to three RM gives you pure strength. In the four- to eight-RM range you develop mostly strength and some muscle mass, while in the eight to 12 and 12-15 ranges you develop strength, muscular endurance and muscular mass. Doing 15-30 RM develops more muscular endurance and less muscular mass and strength. Over 30 RM produces mostly muscular endurance and, if the number of repetitions is sufficiently high, cardiovascular endurance.

In the early stages regardless of your sport, you should train for strength and endurance. After this phase your strength training becomes more specific. For example, if you are a marathon runner you would work mainly on muscular endurance separately and in conjunction with cardiovascular endurance. If you play the backfield in football, you would need to train for speed-strength, strength, and special speed to play well the entire game.

Figure 10.13: Squat with Active Cord

The common theory in weight training is to use heavier weights for greater strength and mass. But, speed-strength, strength endurance, speed and explosive strength are best developed with submaximal weights. Even 50 percent or less of your maximal weight can be used effectively for faster and more explosive execution of an exercise. Maximal weights should be used sparingly.

When strength training becomes specific you need more sets for greater amounts of energy expenditure to create a stronger training effect. But doing more sets in the early stages of training can lead to overtraining, soreness, poor technique and other negative consequences.

In all strength training programs be sure that you are well-prepared physically for the exercises so that you can correctly perform them. Use only the amount of weight that allows you to execute the exercise correctly with good form and without chance of injury.

For example, I have had hundreds of athletes tell me how they can't squat because of a bad back or knees that were injured in the early stages of doing the squat. When they learned how to do it correctly, they realized it was their poor technique coupled with heavy weights that caused the injuries. They now understand that they did not have the ability to do the exercise correctly. Thus, beware of "experts" who recommend heavier and heavier weights. Train wisely, not heavy with pain, soreness and the likelihood of injury.

General (Base) Training

Before doing serious strength training or working specifically for speed-strength or explosiveness, it is important that you have an all-around strength base together with all-around conditioning. This includes not only strength training, but training for flexibility, agility, technique, cardiovascular endurance and other physical qualities. This should be the first phase of your annual training program.

An all-around strength/conditioning base is extremely important to help prevent injury and to enable you to do the more intense specialized explosive and speed training which follows. In general, the exercises become more complex, more intense and more specialized the closer you get to the competitive season.

In the early stages of training and especially for novices, you should do 15-20 exercises in a typical workout to cover all the major joints and muscles of the body. Because of the need for many exercises, only one set for approximately 15-20 RM should be completed. Doing this develops base strength and muscular endurance, and as an extra bonus, you get stronger ligaments and tendons that create more durable joints.

General strength conditioning is subdivided into three major areas: the lower body (legs and hips), the midsection (abdomen and lower back), and the upper body (shoulders, chest, back, arms, hands and fingers). Each of these areas must be well-developed to get the best results in your later training. Athletes have a tendency to ignore or minimize the midsection, but it is needed to make leg and arm actions more effective.

For example, the squat can only be as successful as the midsection is strong. If you cannot support a barbell on the shoulders and hold the normal spinal curvature when doing the squat, it matters little that your legs and arms are strong. In addition, a weak midsection will not allow the force of the legs to be transmitted to the arms, as for example, when throwing or hitting.

The following are basic exercises that you should do for all-around strengthening of the body. Other exercises can be used to bring your weak areas up to par or to further improve your strong areas. If you have had any injuries, you should also emphasize exercises that involve the same muscles, ligaments and tendons, especially as they are used in your sport.

Lower-Body Exercises

Ankle Joint Exercises

1. Heel raises with Active Cords or on a calf raise machine.

2. Seated heel raise with Active Cords or on a seated calf raise machine.

3. Toe raises with Active Cords or on

Figure 10.14: Toe raises on a Tib Exerciser

   special machines such as the Tib Exerciser (Figure 9-14).

4. Ankle adduction/abduction with Active Cords.

Knee Joint Exercises

1. Leg (knee) extensions with Active Cords.
2. Leg (knee) curls with Active Cords or on a leg curl machine.
3. Squat with a barbell or dumbbells in the hands.
4. Delay squat (with holds and slow movements) as in #3.

Hip Joint Exercises

1. Hip extension (on the Yessis Back Machine or a high bench with and without Active Cords).
2. Hip flexion (knee drive) with Active Cords beginning with the thigh behind the body.
3. Hip adduction with Active Cords beginning with the leg out to the side about 30-45 degrees and pulling in toward the body center line – do not cross the body!
4. Hip abduction with Active Cords beginning with the leg directly below the body.
5. Good morning with dumbbells or barbell.
6. Lunge with and without Active Cords, dumbbells or barbell.
7. Side lunge with and without Active Cords, dumbbells or barbell.
8. Glute-ham-gastroc raise. The only exercise that contracts the hamstrings from both ends in sequence. This exercise is executed on the Yessis Back Machine (also known as the Glute-Ham-Developer), and is most important for the prevention and reha-

Figure 10.15: The glute-ham-gastroc raise

bilitation of hamstring injuries. This exercise improves your running, cutting and Olympic lifts as well (Figure 10.5).

9. Medial/lateral hip rotation with Active Cords while seated with the leg straight.

Abdominal

1. Sit-ups (curl-ups) with knees bent, feet on the floor. For more difficult execution, use the Yessis machine or a bench with an assistant.

2. Reverse sit-ups with legs bent, feet off the floor and arms overhead when sufficiently strong.

3. Reverse trunk twist with legs bent or almost straight for more difficulty.

4. Russian twist on the Yessis Back Machine or sturdy table (Figure 10.16).

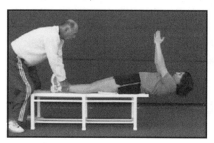 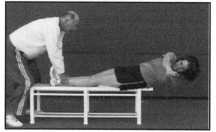

Figure 10.16: Russian twist on the table.

Lower Back

1. Back raises on a Yessis Back Machine or on a sturdy table with an assistant to hold down your legs. This is the best exercise for strengthening the lower back muscles through a full range of motion (Figure 10.17).

 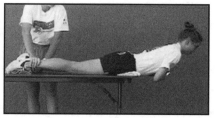

Figure 10.17: Back raise

2. Back raises with a twist in the top position.

3. Reverse back raises.

4. Back (shoulder) twists (advanced).

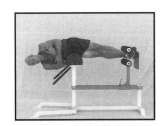

Abdominal/Back Exercises

1. Side bends with Active Cords or a dumbbell in one hand.

2. Side bends on a Yessis Back Machine (Figure 10.18).

3. Side bends on a 45-degree bench (intermediate level).

Figure 10.18: Side bend on the Yessis machine

Upper-Body Exercises

Chest, Back and Shoulder Exercises

1. Bench press with dumbbells/barbell (two to three different grips).

2. Lat pull-down or pull-up (two to three grips and hand positions).

3. Two-way overhead press with dumbbells (neutral and pronated grips).

4. Reverse fly, bent over dumbbell row or standing row with Active Cords.

5. Front arm raise with dumbbells (full range overhead).

6. Lateral arm raise with dumbbells (full range overhead).

7. Overhead front and side pull-downs.

8. Pullover with straight arms (Figure 10.19).

9. Cable crossover, with three to four positions and angles of pull.

Figure 10.19:Pullover with Active Cord

10. Arm forward and side pull-downs from level position.

11. Rotator cuff exercises with Strength Bar, dumbbells and Active Cords.

Figure 10.20: Grip exer-

Arm and Hand Exercises

1. Biceps curl with barbell or dumbbells.

2. Lying and standing (overhead) triceps extension with dumbbell, barbell, Active Cords or cable.

3. Triceps push-down with supinated and pronated grips.

Figure 10.21: Thumb strengthening

4. Wrist curl.

5. Reverse wrist curl.

6. Supination-pronation with Strength Bar.

7. Finger and hand exercises with Exer Rings (Figures 10.20 and 10.21).

Sample Weight Training Day

Start all workouts with active stretching to prepare the muscles for action. Strength exercises are not in any specific order:

1. Heel raise, 1 set of 15-20 repetitions (1 x 15-20).

2. Leg (knee) extension, 1 x 15.

3. Four-way hip (adduction, abduction, flexion, extension), 1 x 15-20.

4. Back raise, 1 x 15.

5. Sit-up (45 degree), 15-25.

6. Back raise with twist, 1 x 8 (count on one side).

7. Reverse sit-up, 20-35.

8. Lateral arm raise, 1 x 15.

9. Front arm raise, 1 x 15.

10. Reverse fly (or bent over row), 1 x 10-15.

11. Reverse trunk twist, 1 x 30 (count on one side).

12. Bench press, 1 x 15.

13. Glute-ham-gastroc raise, 1 x 10-15.

14. Squat, 1 x 15-20.

15. Pullover, 1 x 10.

16. Lat pull-down, 1 x 15.

17. Biceps curl, 1 x 10-15.

18. Triceps pushdown, 1 x 15.

19. Supination-pronation, 1 x 10 on both sides.

20. Wrist flexion (curl), 1 x 15 (with dumbbells).

21. Wrist extension (reverse curl), 1 x 15 (with dumbbells).

22. ExerRings for finger work and grip. Maximum reps. with correct tension ring.

23. Toe raise, 1 x 15.

24. Cable crossover, 1 x 15.

25. Overhead press, 1 x 15.

26. Good Morning, 1 x 15.

Not all exercises have to be done in one session. Training should last no more than one hour; for advanced athletes, up to 2 hours because you will be doing more sets and varying some of the exercises. Most athletes do finger exercises at different times. After doing these exercises for approximately six to 12 weeks you will have an excellent strength base upon which to do endurance, speed, explosive or combinational exercises.

Because of the complexity of strength training and the number of exercises available, not all of the details on their execution could be covered in this book. Instead, the key elements of what constitutes strength and its various forms have been introduced along with guidelines for training. For specific information on the various general and specialized strength training exercises, how they are best executed and for which sports they are best suited, please read the following books by Dr. Yessis: *Kinesiology of Exercise* (and video, *Exercise Mastery*), *Ex-*

plosive Running, Explosive Basketball Training, Women's Soccer: Using Science to Improve Speed and *Explosive Golf,* and the video-DVD *Specialized Strength andExplosive Exercises for Hitting (Baseball, Softball).*

NOTES:

Chapter 11
Speed and Explosive Training

The need for speed and explosive (speed-strength or plyometric) training becomes apparent when you examine the physical needs of most sports. The main movements or skills that you perform are done quickly and usually with great force. For example, athletes who run in their sport (soccer, football, baseball, basketball, lacrosse and rugby) must not only be fast but also be very quick in their maneuverability (agility).

Pitchers, baseball and softball outfielders, shot and discus throwers and javelin throwers must exhibit maximum speed and force in throwing. In these sports the implement is moderately light to heavy and is thrown up to 100 miles per hour. Also included are events that involve only the body, such as the long jump, high jump and vertical jump.

Even weightlifters are explosive in their movements with very heavy weights. Boxers and martial artists must be able to deliver quick and explosive punches. Jump shots in basketball must be executed explosively to avoid being blocked. Football, soccer, lacrosse, field and ice hockey players must be able to

Figure 11.1: Shot-put

execute quick cutting actions and accelerate to get to (or away from) their opponent. Tennis players have to execute quick movements to get to the ball.

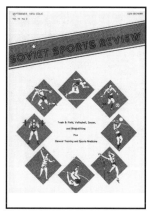

Figure 11.2: Soviet Sports Review

In each case, the key is the speed of limb or body movement. In speed movements which involve rapid changes in the position of the body or body parts, muscle tension is produced by a quick momentary muscular contraction in the preparatory or stopping action, and then reversed, such as in a boxing punch. Such actions may also be repeated at a fast tempo such as in sprinting.

Explosive training consists of plyometric and speed-strength exercises that are executed in 0.15 seconds or less. This is extremely fast, as is the execution of most sport skills. For example, in sprinting the foot is in contact with the ground 0.1 second or less. Half of this time (.05 seconds) is for the landing and half (.05 seconds) is for the take-off. When execution takes more than .15-.20 seconds, it is no longer explosive but it can still be fast. Most throwing and hitting actions take place in 0.2 - 0.3 seconds. However, slower execution of certain exercises is still of value in preparation for explosive training. This includes lead-up plyometric and jump training exercises.

Speed and quickness are determined by your level of strength and the speed with which it is displayed. The ability to display speed and quickness is developed with explosive training. One form of explosive training is **plyometrics**. Although the term plyometrics has been around for over 30 years, it is still generally misunderstood by coaches, athletes and even medical personnel. Many erroneously believe that plyometric training is used to develop strength or is best used as a warm-up. Others believe it is dangerous and will cause injuries.

But **explosive training** or true plyometrics is needed to improve skill execution and game performance, and to prevent injury. The actions involved are powerful and explosive in order to duplicate game conditions. This is the role of true plyometrics and speed-strength training to prepare you for what you must do in game play.

In the late 1960s I was first to report on plyometric training, also known as speed-strength training, a term used by the Russians to identify exercises that displayed strength with speed. The Russians were the first to institute and perfect this type of training. I had many articles on this topic published in the *Soviet Sports Review*, *Sports and Fitness Review International*, and various coaching journals. Articles by U.S. training specialists appeared in the late 1970s, but it was not until the 1980s that books and the popular use of plyometrics appeared.

Sadly, most of the books and videos consisted of jump exercises, not true plyometric exercises. Understand that plyometrics does involve jumping, but all jumps are not plyometric. Most jump exercises such as rope jumping entail long periods of contact with the ground. Jumps in which you go into a deep squat and then jump out of it can take nearly one second to execute (Figure 11.3). Because of this, such exercises are of limited value. They are not true plyometric exercises and should not be called plyometric; they are jump exercises or lead-up plyometrics.

In my travels to Russia, I worked with many Russian specialists, especially Dr. Yuri Verkhoshansky, who created and perfected what we know as plyometrics. He called the training the **shock method**, a derivative of speed-strength training, which I call true plyometrics. Shock training is highly specific and duplicates exactly what the athlete does during the execution of specific competitive skills, such as jumping.

In shock training there must be maximal but quick eccentric muscle contraction loading (tensing), prior to the concentric (shortening) contraction of the muscles and tendons. The shock method, as exemplified in depth jumping, is the purest form of a true plyometric-type exercise. This exercise duplicates the joint and muscle action as displayed in the sports skill.

Figure 11.3: Jump out of a squat

Figure 11.4: T-bench medial rotation ball catches and throws

For example, a speed-strength exercise that duplicates a jumping action seen in the vertical jump is used to develop the ability to execute the jump faster and, as a result, go higher. Or, it could be an exercise to duplicate the arm action in throwing where you receive and repel a ball as quickly as possible. The action involved is the same as in the sports skill. Thus, by doing such exercises you develop the neuromuscular ability to execute the action faster, and as a result, you improve skill execution.

You must create exercises to duplicate the exact action that is involved in each sport. For example, I have developed an exercise that I call the T-bench medial rotation (Figure 11.4). This exercise duplicates what occurs in the shoulder joint of a pitcher when throwing a fastball and other pitches. The exercise can be used to develop the strength of the muscles involved, or when done explosively, to duplicate the quick and powerful action that occurs in the shoulder joint when throwing short and/or long.

Strength is very important in speed and explosive training, but by itself, strength is not the key quality that determines your success in speed-oriented sports (except in adolescence). You must couple the strength with speed for greatest benefit. Only in this way can your strength be used to its greatest advantage.

For example, I worked with a professional football lineman who was brought to me to increase his speed and explosiveness. He was already exceptionally strong, was 6 feet 4 inches tall, and weighed 352 pounds. This was in the early 1980s when the ideal lineman was about 280 pounds. After about five weeks of intense explosive training, he was as fast and as quick as the best linemen on the team (according to team testing) who weighed much less. His weight decreased to 325 pounds and he had 255 pounds of lean muscle mass – more than I have ever seen with other athletes!

At this time, he was capable of leaping up to the top of a table with only arm power. Most important for his position, defensive guard, was not how much he could bench press but how quickly he could execute arm extension. His speed-strength capabilities which allowed him to execute explosive arm actions were the key to his hitting, blocking and tackling movements. Sadly, his coach could not recognize his talent, as he was blinded by the myth that you cannot be fast if you weigh over 280 pounds.

Lead-up plyometrics, also known as preparatory plyometrics, involve jump exercises to prepare you for true plyometric and explosive exercises. They entail easy hopping, skipping, jumping, leaping and bounding. The intensity (height, distance and speed of execution) when doing these exercises is low. Because of this, they are excellent exercises for youngsters and athletes first getting started. Note that most plyometric books and videos published in the U.S. contain mostly lead-up exercises. You can benefit from these exercises if you have never done them before, but they are of little value to a high-level performer who needs explosive training.

Jump training, a form of speed-strength training, is similar to preparatory plyometrics in which you execute moderate to high intensity or high repetition jumps. In jump training, jumps are usually done for maximal height or explosiveness using many repetitions. They are good for repeatedly executing jumps as high as possible. Jump training is used mainly to increase eccentric strength, to prepare the muscles for more intense training, and to work on individual actions involved in the jump, such as quick ankle extension. If the jumps are done explosively and executed as quickly as possible (0.15 seconds or less), then they are true explosive, plyometric jumps.

The term **power** is often used as a substitute for explosiveness. If used in its full sports meaning, it can be a substitute for speed-strength or explosive training. However, the sport of powerlifting has altered the definition of power to mean the lifting of extremely heavy weights.

Figure 11.5: Preparing to accelerate the arm

The heavier the weight, the greater the "power" exhibited. Technically this is a partial truth, but it is not the explosive power that requires speed and quickness. In explosive movements you overcome a resistance or perform a skill in the shortest amount of time. This is the true meaning of power.

To illustrate, it is necessary to examine the definition of power as found in physics — the amount of work done in a certain period of time. Written in formula form it is $P = F \times D/T$, where P is power, F is force, D is distance and T is time. Since speed (S) is equal to distance (D) divided by time (T), power is equal to force times speed ($P = F \times S$). When dealing with the body, only the muscles can produce force. Thus, power equals strength x speed, a speed-strength (explosive) event or strength exhibited with speed.

For example, if you lift a 200-pound weight two feet (as in a bench press) in one second, the power generated is equal to 400 foot-pounds per second. If you lift the same amount of weight and execute the lift in 0.5 second, you exhibit 800 foot-pounds of power! Moving 200 pounds in less than a second may seem extraordinary, but keep in mind that weightlifters apply the majority of their force in less than one second when executing the Olympic lifts. For example, the jerk takes approximately 0.2 seconds.

From this illustration, it becomes clear that significantly more power is generated if there is a faster execution time. Thus there are substantial differences in lifting heavy weights at a slow speed and lifting them at a fast speed. The greatest power achieved in the execution of a particular skill is always a compromise between great force and great speed, rather than a maximization of one at the expense of the other.

When a movement is executed in an explosive manner, it continues on its own inertia. It does not require the steady application of force to keep the object in motion. In complex skills such as throwing and hitting that require multiple joint actions, each has its own periods of acceleration and deceleration. As a result, speed-strength or explosive sports are always associated with high levels of neuromuscular coordination since the movements are usually of a compound nature. They do not involve only one or two joint actions as typically occurs in bodybuilding and powerlifting exercises.

There are two types of speed an athlete usually requires: **running speed** and **speed of limb and trunk movements**. Running speed is determined by stride length and stride frequency, which in turn is determined by limb speed and explosive power. Stride length refers to how much ground you cover in one stride, while stride frequency refers to how many strides you take per unit of time.

For most runners increasing stride length is most important. Once the optimal stride length is reached, improving stride frequency becomes the key factor for increasing speed. To improve running speed, you must first perfect running form with specialized technique, strength and explosive exercises. I recommend *Explosive Running* and *Women's Soccer: Using Science to Improve Speed* for additional information on this topic (Figures 11.6 and 11.7).

To improve speed of leg movements for running, jumping and kicking, or arm movements for throwing and hitting, you should do specialized strength and explosive exercises that duplicate the exact joint actions. In order to increase speed you must apply more force to each individual limb action. As a result, as you create more total force to develop more speed, you also become more explosive.

Overspeed training entails performing a movement faster than usual. It involves neuromuscular training to enable the body to perform faster. There are various methods of overspeed training which are used together with or after speed and explosive training. These include downhill running on a slight incline, the use of

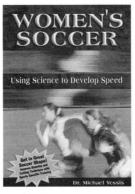

Figure 11.6 and 11.7: Women's Soccer and Explosive Running

weighted clothing, pulling devices and the use of heavier and lighter weights.

Many coaches use **weightlifting** (snatch, clean and jerk) and supplementary weightlifting exercises such as power cleans in explosive training. Weightlifting exercises are explosive in nature and are good examples of speed-strength. Athletes who specialize in weightlifting are some of the fastest athletes in the world. Because weightlifting exercises require strength with speed they can be of value in training an athlete.

However, doing these exercises does not ensure maximum development of your speed-strength qualities in other sports. Even world-class weight-lifters must do supplementary speed-strength exercises, including plyometrics, to improve their explosiveness and quickness. Merely doing Olympic lifts does not insure an increase in speed or quickness in your sport. You may, however, gain an increase in jump height.

For more information on speed and explosive training, see *Explosive Running, Women's Soccer: Using Science to Improve Speed* and *Explosive Basketball Training*.

NOTES:

Chapter 12
The Need for
Endurance

Endurance usually implies cardiovascular endurance, but it can also be muscular endurance, respiratory endurance, psychological endurance—or a combination of several. For example, cardiovascular and respiratory endurance are the key factors in long-distance racing, regardless of whether it is cycling, running, swimming, skating, skiing, rowing or other cyclical-type events. Your performance depends upon your ability to supply the active muscles with adequate amounts of oxygen and essential food nutrients for energy, while at the same time eliminating heat, carbon dioxide and other waste products.

Well-developed cardiovascular and respiratory systems also play a role in strength and maximum speed events, but during the recovery, not the performance. For example, after a 20-, 40- or 100-yard run, you must have the ability to quickly recover and return to the normal (homeostatic) body condition as quickly as possible.

If there is a long period between events, fast recovery is not critical. But if you play a sport such as tennis, lacrosse or soccer, where

Figure 12.1: Tennis backhand

you have bouts of quick, explosive movements followed by periods of relative relaxation, you must have the ability to recover quickly to prepare for the next movements. In such cases the cardiovascular and respiratory systems must quickly remove the waste products, and bring in and create new energy supplies so that you can continue to perform well.

Repeated explosive power or speed bouts also require strength endurance so that your muscles can exhibit a consistent level of performance. Muscular endurance is important in long-distance events in which there are no rest periods, while strength endurance is important in short-time efforts during which you recover before performing again. An example is when a basketball player executes jump shots or a volleyball player executes spikes or blocks. These skills are performed intermittently with periods for recovery. In a marathon, you must have the muscular endurance to maintain your form and to keep the legs moving forward and backward through the same range of motion to maintain your speed for the entire race.

In some cases, combinations of continuous and intermittent performances occur, such as a tennis player involved in a long rally where he or she must continue to execute powerful arm and/or total body movements without any break periods. A lacrosse or soccer player may have to run up and down the field several times without stopping while receiving, passing or going for the ball.

Regardless of your event, there is always a need for psychological toughness to play on the highest levels. This means that you must have the motivation and the psychological endurance in the face of increasing discomfort, pain or discouragement. In general, developing psychological endurance occurs together with the strength and endurance training.

Figure 12.2: Beach volleyball serve

Development of the cardiovascular and respiratory systems (commonly known as the aerobic system) is important for all athletes for improved performance, regardless of whether it is in recovery or the ability to perform well over a long period of time. Although you can improve your aerobic capabilities by participating in endurance sports such as running, cycling or skiing, you should also train to develop the cardiovascular and respiratory systems as needed in your particular sport.

Figure 12.3: Cross-country skiing

Understanding Your Energy Sources

The key to training specificity is to determine which is the predominant energy source for your event. Understand that a constant supply of energy at any and all levels of performance is what determines playing success or failure. The energy sources are different at different work intensities and if your body is not capable of producing and using sufficient energy to maintain performance at the level needed, you will have to stop or slow down to a point where your energy output equals energy input.

Energy for performing your sports activity comes from aerobic, anaerobic and mixed aerobic and anaerobic sources. Aerobic means that the energy is produced in the presence of oxygen. In other words, oxygen is needed to oxidize the products to create the energy. This is the most efficient system for energy production.

Anaerobic means in the absence of oxygen; in other words, work is done relying on the energy sources already stored in the body or, more specifically, in the muscles and liver. However, the amount of stored energy is very small and you cannot perform at peak levels longer than approximately 10 seconds. This energy (your ATP stores) is immediate energy which is used when you first get started, and when you require bursts of high speed or great effort, as in weightlifting.

Most sports events call upon the aerobic and anaerobic systems for the production of energy independently and together. Imagine these energy sources as being on a continuum: aerobic at one end and anaerobic at the other end, with mixed aerobic and anaerobic in between.

The aerobic source is the predominant system. Its basis lies in bringing in oxygen for the production of energy. As the work intensity increases, you tap into the anaerobic system together with the aerobic system. They both supply energy at this time. As you continue increasing the intensity of the workout, you go into the anaerobic zone which uses the stored energy together with the mixed and aerobic systems. When you drop the intensity of the workout, you go back to relying on the aerobic system for recovery and generation of new energy supplies.

Just to go out and perform your activity and have a "good workout" is out of date. If you are a smart athlete you plan your work very carefully to make sure that you are getting maximum benefit from your training program. You work specifically, abiding by what is known as the specificity of training effect. In other words, you train precisely for the results you desire.

For example, if you are trying to improve your aerobic capabilities, you must train in the aerobic zone. If it is anaerobic, it is necessary to train in the anaerobic zone, and if mixed, in the aerobic/anaerobic zone. Only in this way will you be able to attain the needed effect. The three energy sources are required for optimal performance of all athletes and are interrelated; each has an effect on the other and must be in balance.

For example, when you are doing an all-out sprint, it does not mean that only the anaerobic system is functioning. The aerobic system is still operating, but it is not operating at a level that will give you much benefit. Energy for an all-out sprint now comes from the anaerobic system and the breakdown of ATP or stored energy supplies.

Development of the three energy supply systems allows for the maximum development of any one. For example, it is impossible to get maximum development of the aerobic system without also having optimal development of the mixed and anaerobic systems. Therefore, the optimal in long-distance or long-duration endurance events is the proper relationship between all three energy systems, but mostly aerobic. In sports requiring short bursts of speed and continuous playing, your aerobic, mixed and anaerobic capabilities will determine your success.

In practice it is very difficult to determine exactly which is the predominant system operating to supply your energy. The use of heart rate (pulse), speed, performance times and subjective feelings is not adequate for objective evaluation of the training load on your body. In addition, they are not accurate for determining the aerobic, mixed or anaerobic zones in which the work occurs.

Figure 12.4: Cycling

On the highest levels of performance, athletes now use lactate levels to determine energy zones. Understand that as you perform the activity, lactic acid is produced as a by-product of the chemical processes that occur in your body. When in the aerobic zone, lactic acid is used up in the formation of additional energy. Thus, the production of lactic acid and the use of lactic acid are more or less balanced. However, as you move into the anaerobic systems, the production of lactic acid increases much faster than your body can utilize or eliminate it. When the lactic acid levels become sufficiently high, they literally poison the systems and shut down your ability to perform.

To determine your anaerobic threshold, the point at which you move into the mixed zones, be cognizant of the physiological changes that occur as you approach your upper limit of aerobic ability. Determine the changes that occur or the deflection point at which your body is no longer able to metabolize lactic acid at the same rate it is being produced. Most often this is when there is an abrupt change in the breathing rate and oxygen supplies are inadequate to produce the necessary energy at a certain speed or heart rate. You begin to feel uncomfortable as the muscles begin to use energy anaerobically. Your breathing levels rise, your arms and legs begin to feel rubbery and you are forced off your pace and have to slow down.

By training at or near this level several times a week, you can become accustomed to the discomfort and adapt to it as your body tissues become better equipped to clear away the accumulated lactic acid. You receive substantial fitness gains as you improve your ability to train at higher lactate levels and sustain higher power. This is why slow running is not productive. Slow running is good for recovery but not for developing your aerobic system, especially if you want to have the fastest race possible for the distance.

The greater the efficiency and output of your energy supply and the longer you can sustain it, the better will be your speed or performance. The key to performing faster and longer is being able to produce a higher energy output and increasing the efficiency of the energy supply mechanisms. This should be the goal of your endurance training.

A classic example of athletes in great aerobic/anaerobic condition possessing the ability to recover quickly was the former Soviet volleyball team when they dominated world competition. I accompanied them from Long Beach to San Diego where they were to play the American volleyball team that evening. We arrived in the early afternoon at which time the coaches requested an open field to play soccer. It was a full-length soccer field, and when the ball went out of bounds the players had to run after it and put it into play without stopping play.

I stood on the sidelines watching them along with some television sports reporters who were eager to interview the coach and some of the players. They kept asking me to get the coach's attention so they could film and talk to him. After playing for about 30 minutes, I asked the coach if he was ready for an interview. He looked at his watch and said, "No, now we change sides." They proceeded to play for another 30 minutes, after which they went back to their rooms to get cleaned up and to rest.

In the evening, they played as though they had not done any physical activity during the day and easily beat the American team. This is a classic example of how quickly they could recover after doing an all-out endurance-type activity and still perform with explosive power and endurance in the evening.

Training for Cardiovascular and Respiratory Endurance

The main method used to develop the cardiovascular and respiratory (aerobic) systems involves working at a level below your anaerobic threshold pace for long distances or periods of time. For most athletes, this is done by running long distances while staying in the aerobic zone that produces a training effect. For variety, some athletes do cross-country skiing, cycling, swimming or other forms of cross-training. In essence, you should do the activity for a long period of time at a fast enough pace to tax the systems, but without going into the anaerobic range except for short spurts usually at the end.

To participate successfully in an endurance activity, you must also have muscular endurance. You cannot go for long distances if your muscles are not capable of executing the work needed to keep the limbs working for the distance.

Many if not most endurance athletes lack muscular endurance mainly because it does not increase at the same rate as aerobic endurance. This is critical near the end of a race. For example, marathon runners and triathletes who do not have sufficient muscular endurance cannot maintain stride frequency and especially stride length during the run. They are hardly able to bring the thigh forward or push off up with sufficient force. Instead of looking like runners they appear to be shufflers.

The same holds true of the respiratory system. Studies show that when fatigue sets in, the respiratory system gives out before the circulatory system. Thus, you must have endurance of the respiratory muscles for both inhalation and exhalation to prevent the onset of fatigue, and this requires specific training.

To increase muscular endurance, do specific strength exercises for high numbers of repetitions. For example, when you do 50 or more squats without stopping, you will be strongly taxing the cardiovascular system. All repetitions require a combination of muscular endurance and cardiovascular and respiratory endurance. In such cases you cannot separate the cardiovascular and respiratory systems from the muscular system.

In sports that require moving the legs forward on each stride (running, skating and cross-country skiing), it is necessary to do exercises such as the knee drive with Active Cords to strengthen the hip flexors as they are used in the skill execution. With a sufficiently high number of repetitions, you develop the endurance of these muscles to maintain good form and most importantly, to maintain speed for the entire distance.

Sports that require a combination of strength, muscular endurance and cardiovascular and respiratory endurance include the 400- to 1500-meter events. These are not pure strength activities nor are they endurance activities. They require a combination of both and are more accurately known as speed-endurance or strength-endurance activities.

In sports such as basketball and volleyball, you must have strength endurance to be able to jump as high at the end of the game as you do at the beginning of the game. In contact sports such as football, many players become fatigued because of the contact as opposed to the actual physical exertion, since players are in action for only about 15 minutes of an entire game. But they must be able to perform as well at the end of game as at the beginning. This requires a combination of adequate strength, power, muscular endurance and cardiovascular and respiratory endurance.

When running a race such as the marathon, you should be able to maintain the same pace for the entire distance and still have some energy near the end for a "big kick." To do this requires muscular endurance, cardiovascular and respiratory endurance and some power (speed-strength).

For example, a world-ranked long-distance marathon runner whom I helped did many specialized strength exercises as outlined in *Explosive Running*. She did these exercises in lieu of running, which she was unable to do because of medical problems. Prior to the New York Marathon, she had about one to two weeks of running, and then took second place in the race in her age bracket. She told me later that this was her best ever run because she maintained the same speed for the first 22 miles. Fatigue set in during the last four miles and her speed then decreased.

It was the first time in her life that she was capable of running each mile at the same pace. The reason was that she developed sufficient muscular endurance to allow her to run at a steady pace for such a long distance. You will find this is true of most world-class runners, swimmers, skaters, cyclists and other athletes who participate in endurance-type activities. They are capable of maintaining the same pace or close to it for the duration of the race.

Development of the cardiovascular and respiratory systems is very important in youth. However, studies have shown that running long distances or participating in an activity for long periods of time is not always most effective. In the early years your body has a natural tendency to stop after short bouts of all-out activity. Youngsters usually go all-out for a certain period of time and then stop to recover, then repeat the explosive activity and so on. Even though the activity is intermittent, they still develop the cardiovascular and respiratory systems. Studies prove that participation in intermittent types of sports, such as tennis, badminton, soccer, lacrosse, hockey is also effective for the development of the aerobic and anaerobic systems.

Participation in an endurance activity for cardiovascular and respiratory system development should be done during the general preparatory period well before competition begins. Gradually and continuously increase distance or length of time of the activity if you are an endurance athlete. If you are a dual or team athlete you should perform the endurance training for one to three months or more. Then reduce the distance or length of time of the activity and increase the intensity (speed). The increase in speed usually takes place as you move into the specialized training period.

In order to provide a training effect and to ensure that you are developing the aerobic system, the heart rate for a healthy, young, well-trained athlete should be about 150-160 bpm (beats per minute). If you are in the 160-180 bpm range, you will not be able to participate longer than a few minutes, since you will then be taxing both the aerobic and anaerobic systems.

When your heart rate is above 180, the work is performed anaerobically and you must rely on the energy stores in your body. Such activities usually last about 10 seconds, the approximate amount of time you have for maximum burning of your ATP stores. Once ATP is depleted, you must slow down and drop into the mixed aerobic/anaerobic or aerobic zone to get more oxygen for the production of more energy (ATP).

When doing endurance training such as running, we have found the following guidelines to be effective for most team athletes: 1.5 miles, 10 minutes; 2 miles, 14 minutes; 3 miles, 22 minutes For a good rating, you must execute these distances as follows: 1.5 miles, 8:30 minutes; 2 miles, 12 minutes; 3 miles, 18:30 minutes. As you begin the specialized training period, the distances are decreased, but you still do an easy run of up to two miles for relaxation and recuperation after heavy workouts or on the day following a heavy workout.

In the specialized training period, your sport usually demands greater mixed aerobic/anaerobic and anaerobic system development. Thus you should do interval training in the form of short all-out work periods followed by specified rest periods. Wind sprints and various forms of short sprints are very effective at this time.

The following drill has proven successful for interval training: Sprint 110 yards then jog back to the starting position in 1 minute, 15 seconds This is the total time for the sprint and jog back for a total distance of 220 yards, and constitutes one repetition. Do 8-10 repetitions. This is followed by 8-10 repetitions of 75-yard sprints in 50 seconds, for a total distance of 150 yards. Then complete 8-10 repetitions of 55-yard sprints in 40 seconds (total distance, 110 yards). And last, do 8-10 repetitions of 40-yard sprints in 30 seconds, which includes recovery rests, for a total distance of 80 yards.

These workouts can be modified to fit your needs and those of your sport. For example, for greater speed you should decrease the distances and increase the recovery times. The reason for this is that speed development requires more complete recovery. Do short sprints with little recovery for anaerobic development but not for speed, which should follow development of your aerobic and anaerobic systems.

In endurance events, it is wise to train specifically for the race or event that you will be doing. For example, when training for a marathon, long, slow distance running may be effective for the aerobic system development, but to run a fast race, you must run close to your anaerobic threshold. This means you must perform close to the upper limit of your aerobic zone.

For example, if a heart rate of 165 bpm is the upper limit of your aerobic zone, going above 165 bpm will force you into the mixed zone.

The higher the heart rate the more involved will be the anaerobic system. Thus, to train to run as fast a race as possible while still staying in the aerobic zone, you should train with the heart rate just below 165 bpm. This is also an effective range for using fats as your main source of energy.

Train yourself to expend energy at the level needed so that you can have the fastest race possible. Training below this level will not enable you to run faster or to have a higher heart rate or greater aerobic efficiency when trying to perform faster. Training is very specific. You must train for what you will experience.

In team sports, this often means training harder than what you experience in competition. For example, when playing soccer and often when playing basketball, lacrosse or tennis you must continually execute quick bursts of speed with very short intervals of rest in between. Thus, you should train with more multiple bursts of speed for longer periods than you would encounter in a game. This prepares you for the rigors of the game and will make your playing seem easier.

NOTES:

Chapter 13
Agility/Quickness

gility, the ability to make quick changes in direction while in motion, is extremely important in most sports. The quicker and sharper the changes in direction, the better you can not only elude your opponent, but also keep up with him or her. For example, in football there are many good running backs who can run fast in a straight line, but to be great they must also be able to elude their opponent by changing direction quickly. If they do not have this ability, they usually get tackled short of the yardage they could have achieved. Defenders who lack the ability to change direction quickly usually lack the ability to keep up with an opponent who can then free himself to receive a pass or to keep running for more yardage.

The importance of agility for football players can be illustrated by a high school athlete I trained. He won the San Diego regional 100-yard and 200-yard sprints and played some high school football. He was great when it came to running on a track but he lacked the ability to execute cutting actions. We worked on this for several months until he could make quick changes in direction. He then went to a major combine for testing as a wide receiver. He was up against players from USC, UCLA and other universities of equal caliber, while he had only one year of junior college experience.

At the end of the testing, he came in first in the agility tests. He was able to make such sharp and quick changes in direction that he was at least three to five feet away from his opponent when he caught every pass. The defensive backs were amazed at his ability to elude them. The only problem was that the coaches did not recognize him for his ability and only looked at his height, which was below what they considered necessary for a pro receiver.

In basketball, the ability to make quick changes in direction is especially important when trying to get free to receive a pass, or to make a shot or simply to stay with your opponent when he makes a fast break. Quick changes in direction are the key to breaking away from your opponent and staying with your opponent on defense. This ability is especially rewarding when you are able to elude your opponent quickly and drive in for a basket.

For example, I worked with a basketball player who played well in college but was unable to make a professional team. In one year, after improving his cutting technique and physical abilities associated with cutting actions, he was playing on a par with or just below the NBA level and was one of the quickest in the league. No one was able to stop him on his way to the basket, and on defense he was able to shut down all his opponents. The same can happen to you.

Sports such as swimming, track and field and weightlifting do not require much agility. In these sports, the activities are "programmed" so that you do the same thing each time. You do not have to continually change body positions after the movements are perfected, or react

Figure 13.1: Skiing

to changing situations as required in the other sports. This does not mean that you should never train for agility, as there are many instances where it may be needed for self-preservation or unexpected situations. For example, a situation may arise where you have to avoid a collision with another person or avoid a flying object.

The key element in determining the need for agility in a particular sport is whether the sport requires new or different movements

Cinematogram 13.1: Side cutting, right and left

Frame 1   Frame 2   Frame 3   Frame 4   Frame 5

Frame 6   Frame 7   Frame 8   Frame 9   Frame 10

Frame 11   Frame 12   Frame 13   Frame 14   Frame 15

Frame 16   Frame 17   Frame 18   Frame 19

Cinematogram 13.2: Side cut to the right

Frame 1   Frame 2   Frame 3   Frame 4   Frame 5

Frame 6   Frame 7   Frame 8   Frame 9

in relation to changing situations. In almost all team and dual sports there is interaction with other performers and with an object. In such cases, situations arise that many times are quite novel and may require movements and reactions you have never before experienced. The number of such instances is much greater in the early stages of training, but even on the highest levels, after years of practice you may have experienced most situations, but never all. This is why it is important that you continually train for agility, especially if your sport demands it. The agility usually requires quick arm or leg movements as opposed to total body movements. This is usually referred to as specific agility, while total body movements are known as general agility as seen in running and cutting, dodging, stopping and starting.

The Key Components of Agility

To make a change in direction while in motion, especially a quick one, you must have adequate levels of strength (both eccentric and concentric), speed-strength (power), explosive strength, flexibility, co-

Cinematogram 13.3: Side cut to the left

Frame 1   Frame 2   Frame 3   Frame 4

Frame 5   Frame 6   Frame 7   Frame 8

Frame 9   Frame 10   Frame 11

ordination (technique), reaction time and speed of movement. Each of these components can be improved separately or in combination with one another. However, overdevelopment of any one component at the expense of the others will not lead to improvement and may even slow you down.

Most important in agility is coordination, which means having the skill and ability to execute the specific actions required, such as a cutting action when running. This usually means being able to execute basic movements as well as combinations of them.

Learning the cutting technique, the key to agility, requires many repetitions. The specific movement patterns must be practiced over and over, especially as your physical qualities improve. You should practice for five or 10 minutes every morning or afternoon when you are not fatigued so that you can concentrate on the movements that are involved.

Strength and power are also very important to improve agility. Especially important is the eccentric strength needed to make quick stopping and cutting actions when running at high speeds. Concentric strength, when combined with eccentric strength, gives you the power and quickness needed in many actions.

You must also have the range of motion (flexibility) in the joints to execute the skill or movements with maximum effectiveness and efficiency. But going beyond the normal joint range of motion and overstretching the ligament and tendon structures will be a detriment to the movement as it will create a tendency to make bigger and slower movements and weaken the joint. Keep in mind that agility should be displayed very quickly with great forces involved. A weak joint will be susceptible to injury.

Reaction time and speed of movement are usually combined and referred to as response time. Reaction time is the amount of time from the moment the stimulus to act is received to the moment the muscle is stimulated for movement. It may also involve the amount of time for you to make a decision regarding the action you will take. On the elite level, reaction time is reflexive and does not require decision making. Based on your past experiences you automatically respond to a given stimulus which you have experienced many times before.

Speed of movement is the amount of time that elapses from the moment the muscle is stimulated to the moment the action is completed. Speed of movement can be improved, whereas reaction time is innate. Speed of movement is one of the key components of training to develop quickness in arm, hand, leg or foot movements. For improvement in total response time, you should train for an increase in speed of movement.

The level of development of each of these components varies from sport to sport, but as a rule, the highest levels are crucial in sports that require quick changes in movement. This would include individual sports such as figure skating, mogul and slalom skiing. Team sports such as volleyball, basketball, ice and field hockey, lacrosse, soccer, baseball, football, rugby and team handball are also excellent examples of sports that require high levels of agility. It is especially evident in the cutting, stopping and direction-changing actions taken while running, dodging and reacting to changing situations.

Being able to respond effectively to continually changing situations or to initiate changes is a key element in these sports. This is also true in sports such as tennis, handball, badminton, racquetball and squash. All of these sports require very fast starts, stops and quick changes in direction. Without these attributes, it is impossible to be a high-level player.

In individual sports such as gymnastics (especially free exercise), figure skating, acrobatics, diving and skiing, you must be able to change your body positions and posture very quickly for effective and, in many cases, safe performances. Diving, acrobatics, trampolining and free exercise especially demand the ability to combine and change various turns, somersaults and twists in different movements and in different body positions. Sports such as skiing require quick response time to changing slope conditions, as well as the ability to change body-leg positions, especially when slalom skiing.

How to Make Changes in Direction

When making a quick, sharp change in direction while running or skating, it is first necessary to stop your forward motion. The faster you are moving, the more difficult this becomes and the ability to make a sharp change in direction diminishes. However, the stronger you are, the faster you can go and still make a sharp — up to 90 degree — change in direction. This is how improving your physical abilities can improve your performance tremendously.

In order to stop your forward motion (especially when moving fast), you must have great eccentric strength. In essence, the muscles of the leg, especially the quadriceps, undergo a strong quick stretch and lengthen under tension as the knee bends slightly. When the tension becomes sufficiently great, the knee stabilizes and your forward motion stops at the same time. Doing this also stops momentum of the upper body (if you don't lean into the stop) so that you can now make a quick change in direction. See Cinematogram 13.1 for cutting actions to the right and left.

When you plant the foot (leg) in order to stop your forward motion, it should always be placed in a direction opposite the one in which you intend to move. For example, if you wish to make a cutting movement to the right from a forward run, you must plant the left leg out to the left side and lower the body. The plant should also be slightly in front depending upon your speed of approach. The forward and side plant will then allow you to stop your forward motion and place you in an advantageous position to move out to the opposite side. However, the cutting action cannot be very sharp if you are running extremely fast. If you anticipate making a sharp 90-degree cut to the side, slow down so that you can execute the move.

As your left leg is placed on the ground, you must lower your body to become more resistant to changes in movement and to make the stopping action easier and more effective. The more you lower your body, the more stable your body becomes, which then allows you to change your body position to make the directional changes. The taller you remain, the easier it will be to go into motion, but if you try making a quick stop, you will topple over and lose balance. Thus, if you want to go in motion from a stationary position, be as tall as possible, but still maintain a slight crouch. To stop, get the body as low as possible. Lowering the body is usually done by taking a wide step out to the side or forward and letting the body go down, but still keeping the trunk erect.

As you stop and lower the body, begin turning the hips toward the new direction. Your head and shoulders should still remain facing forward so that your opponent cannot read any anticipated changes in direction. As you stop, begin the push-off in the new direction and at the same time turn your head and shoulders in the intended direction of movement. At this time, you should also step out with the right leg, which should be unweighted during the stepping action, in the new direction to prepare to resume running.

After the stop, when the leg you are stepping out with hits the ground, your body should be fully turned so that you are now facing in the new direction with the rear foot breaking or ready to break contact with the ground. This can be seen in Cinematogram 13.1. You are now in the new running stride (see Frame 14). Since you are getting started from a stationary position, the first few strides should be relatively short and you should lean the upper body forward to accelerate. However, after a few steps you should return to your full running stride with an erect body position or prepare for another cut.

It must be stressed that all of the above actions are accomplished in one step. That's right, one step! This is why this technique of executing a cut is so effective in increasing your quickness and your ability to elude your opponent. All too often, I see athletes taking two or three short stutter steps to stop their movement in one direction before stepping out into the new direction. This technique loses valuable seconds. In addition, your opponent is alerted to a change in direction and prepares himself so that he can keep up with you as you make the cut.

If you are on offense and wish to evade your opponent, you should look your opponent in the eye as you step out to the side and lower your body. By looking at your opponent, it will take him longer to realize that you are about to change your direction. This does not preclude you from executing feinting actions to avoid your opponent. These are still effective, but the more you can change how you execute the cut — for example, look him straight in the eye with no head movements or at other times, turn the head in one direction but then cut in the other direction — the more off balance you can keep your opponent and the more effective your movements will become.

All cutting actions should be done on the outside leg. This means the leg that is opposite the direction in which you intend to move. Thus if you are going to cut right, you push off with the left leg to the right. If you are going to cut to the left, you push off with the right leg. When making a change in direction from right to left, you push off with the right and when changing from the left to the right you push off with the left leg.

When making a change in direction while moving forward or backward, you can push off with whichever leg is used to take the last stride before you execute the reverse movement. Thus if you stop and push off with the right leg, you turn to your left; if you push off with the left leg, you turn to the right.

However, if you wish to go to the right and you execute the cutting action off the right leg, not only will it be executed more slowly, but it will never be as sharp as when you do it off the left leg. Very often you will slip if playing on grass because you will not have a solid base. Only the upper lateral border of your shoe will be in contact with the ground during the push-off, as opposed to the sole of the foot when using the opposite leg. In spite of its ineffectiveness, many athletes still use this method for cutting. If you are one of these athletes, I strongly recommend that you make the necessary changes.

In Cinematograms 13.2 and 13.3 we do not see as quick a change in direction as is possible. The girls do not lower the body to indicate fast movement or the need for more stability. They do not step out very far on the first step, indicating a weaker push-off and a slow turn of the body with the swing leg. However, the basic technique is good. They just need greater strength and power in the actions to make the cut faster and more effective.

You can never have too much agility. Continual improvement of this physical quality will always improve total sports performance. It will enable you to respond to changing situations most quickly and effectively. You will be the player who typically steals the ball from your opponent, evades or dodges him, gets the jump on him, intercepts or breaks up various plays or shots, and always seems to get "sure points." You will be the player who comes out of nowhere and appears to be involved in every play. You will carry out your responsibilities and execute play actions most effectively and efficiently.

Beware of many so-called speed and quickness experts who develop "quick feet." They run many drills such as ladder drills, where you must raise the thighs to step over the rungs of the ladder or to step over cones set up in different directions. In all of these drills, you must get the feet off the ground quickly and raise the legs to go over the hurdle or obstacle that is placed in your way. These may be great drills for raising your leg, but understand that agility is not an up-and-down action, it is lateral. Agility stems from the hips, not from the feet. It is more accurate to say that you have quick legs rather than quick feet.

In addition, you must learn how to make changes in direction quickly. If you are not taught to improve this ability, you will never become faster regardless of how many high knee drills you do. In fact, there are many professional athletes who, after getting exposed to these so-called experts, have actually become slower in their cutting actions rather than improving their speed and quickness. Do not fall into this trap.

In addition to learning effective cutting technique, you should also improve the strength and explosive power of the muscles involved in making the cutting actions. Since cutting is tied to running, many of the exercises used in running can also be used to improve your cutting abilities. These include exercises such as the squat, the ankle extension (heel raises), the knee drive, pawback, good morning, and reverse trunk twist.

However, since the cutting action is a lateral-type movement, it is also necessary to perform exercises to strengthen the hip abductors, which are the main muscles involved in executing the cut. To this end you should do hip abduction exercises, which include the side lunge with dumbbells or a barbell and especially with Active Cords to duplicate the exact action involved in cutting. To balance strengthening of the hip abductors you should do adduction exercises on a cable pulley or with Active Cords.

Since the ankle undergoes extreme ranges of motion in a sideward direction, it is also necessary to do foot strengthening exercises with Active Cords to help prevent ankle adduction and abduction. Keep in mind that the ROM undergone by the ankle in a sideward motions of a sharp cut greatly exceeds the range that you can perform on your own accord.

Because the cutting action is executed so quickly, you must do explosive exercises including plyometrics. Some of the better exercises include double-leg side jumps, single-leg side jumps and single-leg jumps forward, backward and to both sides. Also important are exercises such as ankle jumps to isolate the ankle action, which plays an important role in the push-off.

In conclusion, basic cutting technique is the same regardless of whether you are running forward and wish to cut to one or the other side, or whether you only want to make an angle cut while still continuing in a forward direction. The same basic technique applies to running sideways and then changing direction, running to the opposite side or running forward and then stopping and running backward. In essence, each of these different types of cuts include a stopping and body turning action, coupled with a push-off, all executed in one step.

When you master the cutting technique and do exercises to strengthen and make the muscles more explosive, you will be amazed at how much quicker you are in game play. For more details on cutting actions and exercises specific to cutting, see *Women's Soccer: Using Science to Improve Speed* and *Explosive Basketball Training*.

NOTES:

Chapter 14
Flexibility

Flexibility is the range of motion (ROM) exhibited in a joint movement. When you hold a position at the end range of motion for 10-60 seconds it is known as static flexibility. Dynamic (active) flexibility depends on a muscle contraction to move the limb or body part through the ROM. The structural make-up of the joint, the tightness or looseness of the muscles and connective tissue surrounding the joint, including the ligaments and tendons, play a role in the ROM.

Stretching is used to increase flexibility. This includes static, passive, active, dynamic, PNF explosive stretching and combinations of them. Each method has different benefits and some are more important in sports than others. For athletes, the stretching should be used to warm up the muscles, increase the range of useful movement, reduce injury, prevent and alleviate muscle soreness after exercise and increase the level of skill and motor efficiency. To receive these benefits you need active stretching. The other forms of stretching fulfill only one or two purposes and may have some negative affects.

Specific forms of stretching are used for conditioning muscles, tendons and other soft tissues. For example, prolonged slow static stretching can cause permanent deformation of connective tissue and high levels of strain on the muscle. In slow static stretching (which includes Yoga), when there is a slow loading rate, the bony insertion of a ligament or tendon is the weakest component of the bone/soft tissue complex. In active stretching the soft tissues are the weakest components, especially at very fast loading rates as in true plyometrics.

Static stretching is the most popular form of stretching and is simple to learn and easy to execute. The stretches are done by holding a position while trying to increase the ROM and the duration of the stretch for up to 30 or more seconds. The muscles are relaxed and the stretching ROM gradually increases after a number of repetitions. If a partner or some apparatus is used to assist in the stretch (passive stretching), a greater ROM may be achieved, but the potential for injury increases.

For the athlete, static stretching is insufficient to develop the full dynamic ROM that is required. For athletes, stretching should be active and often combined with dynamic strength exercises to condition the muscles and collagenous tissues, increase muscle strength and enhance capillarization and circulatory efficiency.

Active (dynamic) flexibility correlates most strongly with sporting proficiency and resistance to injury, while static and passive stretching only enhance static or passive flexibility. Active flexibility relies on the strength of the muscles or outside forces such as gravity to move the limbs or body part through a full ROM.

For maximum efficiency, you should do strength exercises that also enhance flexibility. Exercises through the full ROM fulfill this objective. For example, in the lateral arm raise exercise, raise the arms to a full overhead position. This involves contraction of the deltoid muscles to move the limbs through the full ROM. The weights create additional resistance so that the muscles gain strength through the full ROM.

Executing a skill such as kicking, throwing or hitting a ball involves active muscle contractions through a full ROM. There is active muscle participation together with the display of flexibility. These are natural movements. Thus, to prepare the muscles and joints for execution of these movements, you should do active stretches.

Active flexibility should be a part of all training. Anytime it is necessary to increase flexibility, the movement should be done through the full ROM with gradual increases in the ROM with each repetition. Movements should be performed to enhance flexibility, and/or strength, speed, local muscular endurance or skill. When you do this, separate stretching sessions become redundant.

At present, most training programs begin with static stretching before progressing to active training exercises. There are even separate static stretch sessions during the training. This universality of static stretching implies that it is a form of physical conditioning which is quite independent of other forms of training. But it is not and should not be considered as such. Only in rare cases where excessive flexibility is needed should static or other forms of stretching be done to increase the ROM that may be impossible to achieve actively.

Children and youngsters are extremely flexible, mainly because the joints and tissues are still developing. Thus, coaches should use active stretches for warm-up! If the youngsters remain active in a wide variety of sports, they usually maintain adequate levels of flexibility. In such cases it is not necessary to execute more stretches unless there is a decrease in the normal ROM or when an increase in flexibility is dictated by the particular sports skill. Working to become more flexible during youth is usually counterproductive, as it may lead to excessive flexibility.

Excessive flexibility creates looser joints, which then become more prone to injury. For example, athletes who religiously practice static flexibility greatly increase the ROM in their joints. At the same time, they start getting more injuries because the support structures that hold the joints together and limit the ROM can no longer do their job.

Thus it is important that stretching be done through the full ROM but not beyond. When doing active stretches with the muscle under contraction through the full ROM, it is almost impossible for you to go beyond the normal range. This is not the case with static or passive stretches, many of which are potentially dangerous because of the overstretching.

For example, the standing toe touch is a common hamstring stretch in which you bend over from the hips and waist to touch the hands to the feet (or floor) while keeping the legs straight. However, most of the stretching in this exercise takes place in the lumbar spine rather than in the hip joint (hamstring muscles and tendons). The muscles of the lower back become relaxed, and support of the spine is provided by the ligaments of the lumbar spine that hold the vertebrae in place.

As you increase the ROM, the relaxed lower back ligaments get extended when this stretched position is held for long periods of time, and as a result, the lumbar spine becomes looser. If the lower back muscles are not strong enough to maintain proper alignment, the spine becomes more susceptible to injury. The same negative results are achieved with the crossed leg, hurdler and seated split-leg stretches.

The standing and seated toe touch stretches are often used to help stretch and relax the lower back muscles and ease pain. Because it feels good, you are lulled into believing that it is a good stretch. In reality, however, the joint capsules in the vertebrae become overly compressed and block the nerves so that no pain is felt. This "good" feeling remains for some time, but several hours later or on the next day, the pain returns. Stretching again only exacerbates the problem.

Other potentially dangerous stretches include:

1. The windmill stretch in which you bend from the hips and waist until your rounded torso is basically level to the ground, and you then rotate the shoulders to alternately touch the hand to the opposite foot.

2. The lying and standing quadriceps stretch in which you bend a leg and pull the foot in close to the buttocks.

3. The shoulder stretch in which one arm is raised overhead and grasped at the elbow with the other hand. The elbow is then pulled toward and behind the head as much as possible.

Active stretching with the muscles contracting through the full ROM results in active muscle control through the full ROM. The contractions prepare the muscle for action and help to prevent injury. The dynamic stretch of a muscle or muscle group brings into play neuromuscular mechanisms which help to activate your coordination and make movements safe and effective. When an active stretch is done with the muscles under contraction through the full ROM, the muscles are prepared in their three different contraction regimes.

For example, the execution of the squat actively stretches the quadriceps, hamstring and buttocks muscles, and uses many other muscles as stabilizers to hold the trunk and legs in place. This, in turn, helps to maintain balance and produce good posture. In such dynamic stretches in which you may also strengthen the muscles or develop aerobic endurance, the muscles are prepared for work while the joint undergoes a full ROM. Thus the squat is a safe exercise and stretch that prepares the hip and knee joint muscles for action in skills such as running, jumping and cutting.

Strength exercises as well as free natural movements can be considered active stretches. For example, standing on one leg while repeatedly raising the other leg in front of the body will actively lengthen and stretch the hamstrings and buttocks muscles. The hip flexor muscles undergo contraction to pull the limb through the full ROM and, together with the hamstrings, are prepared for activity as the dynamic range is increased.

Figure 14.1: Active side bends

Active Stretches for Sports

Before practice or competition, you should warm up and regain your already-developed ROM. Gaining more flexibility at this time should not be an objective. Before competition it is necessary to warm up the muscles and prepare them for the work ahead. The exact amount of active stretching and other preparation varies greatly and depends upon your sport and personal needs.

Since sports skills are very specific, active stretches, in addition to having a general effect, must also be specific to the sports skills involved. This means that the active stretches must duplicate as closely as possible the actual positions and movements that you will experience during the execution of the sports skill. In addition, the stretches

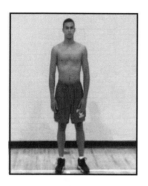

Figure 14.2: Active side lunge

should involve the muscles in the same muscle contraction regime that they undergo in the competitive skill.

If the muscles contract explosively, as in sprinting or jumping, then it is necessary to build up to some plyometric-type stretches to prepare the muscles for the execution of these skills. For example, in sprinting for maximum stride length it is necessary to have a wide forward-backward spread between the thighs in the push-off and airborne phase. To reproduce this position you should do the classic lunge, not a split squat that many athletes call a lunge. Note that the lunge is also used to prepare you for low-reaching movements in sports such as tennis, baseball, basketball and volleyball.

Only you (or your coach) should determine the active stretches you need and how many should be done. Some athletes need more exercises to get ready, while others need less. To help make your decision, experience many active stretches, paying attention to how they feel and how well they duplicate the movements and muscle actions that you need.

For examples of active stretches and their descriptions, see the following books: *Explosive Basketball Training*, *Women's Soccer: Using Science to Improve Speed*, *Explosive Running*, *Explosive Golf*, *Explosive Tennis: The Forehand* and *Explosive Tennis: The Backhand*.

NOTES:

Chapter 15
Balance

Balance is involved in the execution of sports skills and can determine how successfully you perform. In general, balance is developed simultaneously with the exercises and sports skills that you learn and perform. However, in some cases it may require supplementary training, training that must be specific to the skill.

In the sports and fitness fields, balance and balance training are usually included in the now popular "core training." However, such core training may be beneficial for lay people, but does little for true athletes. Balance in athletic performances is dynamic. The balance and core strengthening that is now in vogue is mainly static and thus not related to sports performance.

The balance training, which consists of maintaining basically static poses, does not improve dynamic performance. It may benefit archers and biathletes who must hold a stable position, but it will not assist athletes involved in running and cutting activities or playing sports such as soccer, basketball, hockey, tennis, lacrosse, football and baseball. Static training is of value mainly when the athlete must hold the body or portion of the body in a stationary position.

Combinations of static and dynamic balance are seen with circus acrobats who walk blindfolded on a tight wire, balance on a tiny board mounted on rollers, and ride a unicycle turning the pedals alternately with their arms and legs. Gymnasts who perform various somersaults and twists in free exercise and on apparatuses display great dynamic balance. These athletes have great balance, muscle strength and agility. They develop their sense of balance through training to strengthen not only the muscles but also the various balance mechanisms of the body.

Maintaining balance or stability is extremely important since you are never fixed in one place. Your body is constantly losing and recovering balance as you walk, run, jump, throw, kick — perform just about every physical movement that you can imagine. You require constant readjusting to remain balanced or properly aligned in good posture.

Balance is an intricate process controlled by many different organs and systems. This includes the brain, the control center for the central nervous system, which receives information from the balance mechanisms in the ears, eyes and from receptors in the joints, tendons and muscles. Upon receiving information about the status and vital tonus of the various organs, the central nervous system automatically adjusts your posture and movements by sending the appropriate signals to the muscles.

If you are sick or have an ear infection, there is a loss in your sense of balance which often leads to falls. One of the most common signs of balance loss is dizziness upon changing body or spatial positions, as for example, when swinging on a swing or riding in a vehicle. In addition to feeling dizzy, your sense of well-being may decline, your heart rate may quicken and nausea may set in.

Balance-enhancing exercises can improve coordination, attentiveness, confidence in your strengths and even a degree of daring. To have good control over your body, you must develop the ability to consciously control your equilibrium. Do this by focusing attention on dynamic exercises, especially strength exercises, designed to maintain the proper vertical position of the spinal column. This entails strengthening the muscles of the abdomen, lower back, hip, neck, feet and legs.

To maintain a tall body position, you evoke a reflex action which automatically contracts the lower back muscles to help you stand straight. Thus, posture exercises can have a positive effect on your equilibrium. Also important are exercises performed blindfolded to develop what is known as a muscle or kinesthetic sense. In essence, the muscles learn what it feels like to assume a particular position (posture), which when deviated from, can be easily reassumed.

For active balance development, you should do easy runs with frequent changes in direction (agility) and execute simple acrobatic exercises such as the front roll, side roll and others. Athletes who must control their bodies in space should do jumps with body turns while in the air or execute throwing or shooting actions after a jump and body turn.

For example, I have athletes perform vertical jumps with forward movement and a half or full turn of the body for up to 180 degrees. They must take off and land on the same line as they make forward progress. When first starting, most athletes lose their orientation very quickly. But as they develop better dynamic balance, the intensity of the jumps and other movements increases, so that even greater balance and control of the body in space are developed.

To effectively train the balance mechanisms, perform exercises which involve various trunk bends, head turns and trunk turns while moving with different stride lengths and frequencies. As your execution of these various moves improves, the number of repetitions can be increased.

Static/Dynamic Balance Exercises

The following are a few exercises that you can do to develop both static and dynamic balance. These are sample exercises which can be adapted with a little imagination to create many other appropriate exercises. The exercises should be adapted to your needs based on the sports skills in which you are involved and the type of balance most needed.

1. Stand on one leg, then bend the free leg and place the foot on the knee of the support leg. Place the hands on the waist, then hold them out to the sides or in a forward position. Do the exercise with the eyes open and with the eyes closed.

2. From a standing position raise one leg so that the thigh is parallel to the ground and the knee is bent with the shin relaxed. Rotate the upper body and bend forward to touch the raised knee with the opposite elbow. Hold for 10-15 seconds and then repeat on the opposite side. This exercise can also be done in an alternating manner without holding.

3. Stand on one leg and swing the other leg in various directions. For example, swing the leg upward through a full ROM, then swing the leg downward and backward through a full ROM. Hold the final position after executing the swing. The key to this exercise is to maintain upright body posture and to move the arms in different positions for different levels of balance.

4. The squat exercise is important for balance. Various squat positions, especially on one leg, should be held up to four to five seconds in order to develop the eccentric and isometric strength needed to hold different postures. One example is to raise the free leg forward and hold it there as you squat.

5. The classic side and front lunges are excellent for balance when holding an upright trunk position. This execise can also be executed with the arms directly overhead holding a light pole or bar.

The key to developing balance is to be able to maintain positions in static and dynamic postures during and after movement. For example, jump, imitate an execution of a jump shot or a block, and then land on both feet in a balanced position. Next, take several approach steps, leap up, imitate a movement, land and hold. The exercise can be varied by raising one leg quickly and balancing on the other after landing.

Learn to balance on one leg, especially if you must develop hitting and throwing skills as in tennis, golf, baseball, hockey, lacrosse, soccer and badminton. In these sports you must often execute a throw or hit with most or all of your weight on one leg. Movements to duplicate the hit or throw can then be added to develop balance while in position or to attain balance after the hit or throw.

Stability

Being in a stable, well-balanced position is very important for executing sports skills and doing exercises for strength, speed, power and flexibility. For example, in doing an overhead press, the muscles of the body must contract dynamically and isometrically in order to hold the body in place. If the muscles do not contract to maintain balance, any changes in weight positioning could make you lose balance, resulting in injury.

The basic principles of stability when exercising and playing sports are relatively simple: the larger your base of support, the greater your stability. This is the reason you should assume a position with the feet at least shoulder-width apart for better side-to-side balance. If the feet are close together, you have a small support base, which makes it more difficult to be stable when doing overhead lifts or other exercises. But it is a good position for moving quickly into action. When your feet are in a stride position (one foot in front of the other), there is better balance in a forward/backward direction, but less sideways.

Another way to increase stability is to bend the knees and lean forward (crouch). For example, when assuming a ready position, bend the knees slightly (slight squat) to lower your center of gravity (weight). The lower you are, the more stable and resistant to movement you become. Also, when twisting the trunk with the spine vertical, bend your knees to stabilize the lower body and hips and to isolate the rotation to the shoulders.

In the ready position for fielding in baseball or softball, or for movement in any direction, your center of gravity should be kept relatively high. In such cases it is advantageous to have the knees bent only slightly, with the trunk inclined slightly forward (lowered) from the hips. Lowering the upper body increases stability but still allows you to be in good position for movement with the legs.

Falling

Related to balance is learning how to fall. This is extremely important in many sports ranging from gymnastics to skiing to the martial arts. For example, when first learning to ski you will do much better if you have no fear of falling after losing your balance. As you begin to fall, tuck your body and make contact with the ground over the largest area possible. Go into a roll, or several rolls if needed, after the fall.

Also perform falling exercises: for example, squat into a shoulder roll, or squat, roll over backwards, and then roll sideways. The falls can be followed by quick recovery or can be repeated several times in succession.

Exercises such as these can help improve your overall balance. They enable you to adapt your movements and body positions to changing conditions. In addition, you will be able to execute movements with greater ease and improve your ability to do many skills. No one should be exempt from such balance activities.

You should never undertake exercises from an unstable position, especially exercises for strength. Some trainers advocate trendy balance programs with exercises such as the squat on large, inflated balls. This is extremely dangerous and can easily ruin your knees or injure your spine. Also ill-advised are strength exercises on rollers and wobble boards that can be extremely dangerous.

You should use weights in an exercise only when you are in a balanced, stable position. If you lose your balance, you can more easily regain it during or at the conclusion of the exercise. Balance involves the entire body, not just parts of the body. Do balance exercises that are specific to your sport and not merely for static posture, as the latter will not help you in your sports performance.

NOTES:

Chapter 16
Your Incredible Eyes

Contributed by Dr. Bill Harrison

Keep your eyes on the ball and *see the open player* are commands that are part of most coaches' vocabulary. It is rather easy to do in practice when that is your sole concern. But you can lose your visual focus when you are thinking too much about mechanics, simply concentrating too much or when the game gets fast.

A high percentage of errors on the playing field are preceded by a visual mistake. In competition, athletes frequently take their eyes off the ball, don't attend to important visual cues, are late in their recognition and their field of vision becomes narrow or they lose court and field awareness.

When you see great athletes do incredible things, rest assured the action started with their vision. The same is true when they struggle—a visual breakdown precedes the physical breakdown. Put simply, eye-mind-body (EMB) speed and control is what you're witnessing when you can't believe your eyes—eyes that guide the mind and body. The best of the best in all sports are those who possess the EMB speed and control. From baseball's Barry Bonds to volleyballs' Keri

Figure 16.1: Baseball

Figure 16.2: Tennis

Walsh, the greatest athletes possess extraordinary EMB speed and control.

The best athletes recognize patterns no one else sees. It's a boxer seeing the punches before they become punches, or a football running back seeing holes that exist only for him. More than foot speed or strength or nerve, these phenomenal performances require great EMB speed and control.

Those who possess this quality see their game as a slow motion movie, instead of the slide show that others see. Clearly, the ability to visually slow down the game is an important step in being able to perform well.

The control element of EMB control is as important as speed. Athletes attempting to catch, hit and kick balls are commonly seen missing as their eyes look ahead of the action and not on the ball itself. But you can increase your awareness and appreciation of how your eyes and visual system function and significantly influence your sports performance.

Sports, because of lightning fast actions, require highly developed visual skills. Sports require more than just clear eyesight. To succeed in high-level competition you must have a variety of dynamic visual skills. In sports you are in motion, and the ball and your opponents are in motion, which challenges your visual skills. It's not simply eye-hand coordination or eye-foot coordination, but eye-body coordination that matters, as the eyes act as the body's guidance system.

Your visual skills include fast visual recognition; accurate depth and distance perception to see teammates, opponents and balls moving at very high speeds; accurate tracking of balls breaking in sharp trajectories; and great peripheral vision. Your visual skills must allow you to collect all the visual information, including speed and direction of rotation of the seams of the ball, a slight change in the ball's trajectory and its relative speed at any given moment in time. When done correctly, the ball appears slower than normal.

Because your eyes are open doesn't mean that your vision is functioning. For example, when you are driving but lost in thought, you temporarily go functionally blind. This phenomenon is called "inattentional blindness." It's a scary thought, but most athletes go functionally blind at times. Those moments of temporary blindness can be critical and lead to mistakes on the playing field. It only takes a millisecond of functional blindness to make an error, miss an important cue, etc.

Isn't it amazing that a tennis player can leap across the court and swing a racket at a cannon ball at just the right angle so it darts back into the corner of the court opposite the opponent? How can a quarterback look through and around several tall, wide linemen, see a safety begin a step toward his intended receiver and make the decision to pass to his fullback trailing the play? Why is it that an expert skeet shooter gets 25 straight hits on a windy day as the clay pigeons streak through the air like comets, while you miss more than you hit? Why?

These athletes have learned how to slow down the apparent flight of objects so there is plenty of time to do what seems incredible to the less-gifted and less-highly trained. It's as if the eyes have the power to split a second into a thousand parts.

Your vision will deteriorate when you are in motion. Try holding a newspaper or magazine in your hand while running in place. You will find that your reading skills deteriorate immediately. The faster you run, the more impaired your vision. The same is true in sports.

Your vision is maximally challenged when you play at game speed. The limited amount of time available makes it a significant visual challenge to pick up critical visual cues in time to react properly. You train your body to react with an endless number of beneficial physical drills. Equally important is that you learn how to get the visual information that will trigger your reactions in the high-speed game action. If you don't pick up the visual information quickly and accurately, there is no way you are going to react properly.

In many sports, early recognition and accurate identification are critical. In baseball and softball, the difference between a good

Figure 16.3: Hockey

Figure 16.4: Soccer

pitch to hit and a poor pitch to hit can be very slight. In football, a defensive player's reactions depend on what he sees, and early recognition is vital. Keep in mind that vision is learned, and anything that is learned can be better learned.

A fundamental principle of vision is that you see what you look for. If you don't look for the right things you won't see them, even if they are right in front of you. Seeing with recognition and identification is a very active process. It is a "doing" activity, not just a passive, looking process. When your eyes look at something you must inspect every detail. You can't just aim your eyes at the object, you must always inspect for information. It is similar to what a baby does when he or she is determined to reach a bottle...you give total effort while observing.

Approximately 80 to 90 percent of your actions on the field involve some aspect of vision. Since vision is so involved in your performance, it should be clear that any improvement in the visual system will result in a direct improvement in your performance. With the proper emphasis, it will become apparent that a superior visual system is a key for consistent top performance and yes, most top performers have it.

For example, if you play a sport in which a high speed ball is coming directly toward you, as is the case with a goalie, a hitter, a tennis player etc., one of the most difficult things to do is to time your actions exactly with the velocity of the ball. Timing is critical and is highly dependent upon excellent depth perception. The training of depth perception will result in improved timing and improved performance.

The 14 micro-muscles in the eye and your various forms of eye movements determine the quality of your dynamic vision skills. Your overall quality of sports vision is 100 percent dependent upon how these muscles operate together.

Great athletes in basketball, soccer and football have broad peripheral awareness. They seem to be aware of everything. Controlled rapid eye movements are a contributor to this ability. Visual memory, the ability to maintain an image of what you have previously seen, also enhances peripheral awareness and subsequently field and/or court awareness.

Your sports vision skills can be enhanced simply by being more aware of what you see when you are performing effectively, particularly in competition. A variety of recreational sports activities can be helpful, and specific off-the-field eye drills can be of use as well. Ping pong, handball and punching a speed bag are all good activities for developing faster eye movements and eye-hand coordination. Hacky sack and soccer drills are helpful in developing better eye-foot coordination.

Eye doctors specializing in vision training provide in-office training programs, similar to in-office physical therapy programs. Internet-based training programs are also available and can give you a home training program to further develop your dynamic visual skills, including visual concentration skills, depth perception, control of your eyes, the ability to see while moving, speed of recognition and visual memory (see www.SlowTheGameDown.com). Home training saves you important time, and the portability provided by an Internet-based training program is a significant advantage.

You can improve EMB speed and control with the proper training. You can learn to recognize key information more rapidly, and see things in motion more clearly. You can learn to gauge velocity and velocity changes more accurately, to have greater field and/or court awareness and to have better visual concentration so you can slow down the ball or game. With training you can gain the ability to maintain visual dominance and possess the skills to "slow the game down."

You were born with the capability for great eyesight, but you must work to transform eyesight into vision. If you get lazy you will have lazy vision and your physical abilities will not be achieved.

Your eyes affect your mind and your body's functioning and, conversely, the mind and body's functioning affects your eyes. It is your visual system that provides you the key information to act when you throw, kick or hit; find an opening for a pass or a run; get the jump on an opponent; or are aware of the entire field or court. The various visual skills related to your sport can be trained. No matter what position or what game you play, you will become better by training your eyes and learning how to gain the best use of them. For more information, contact:

Dr. Bill Harrison
Performance Fundamentals, Inc.
1100 S. Coast Hwy., Ste. 203
Laguna Beach, CA 92651
www.SlowTheGameDown.com
(866) 627-5400

NOTES:

Chapter 17
Nutrition for Optimal Playing

If you want to be a great player, you must give your body the right fuels to achieve it. Your diet must satisfy your mouth as well as your muscles, and there is a way of eating that will enhance your playing and health. The only diet you should be on is the one you can stay on and enjoy for life. In essence, your eating habits must be part of your lifestyle.

Supercompensation

Think of food as a very important ally. Why? Because of a simple phenomenon known as supercompensation. It occurs in response to the training effect — when the body undergoes structural changes due to your training. For example, if you work out more than you are used to, your body will experience a greater work load than it is accustomed to. As a result, you deplete your body's en-

Figure 17.1: Food pyramid products

ergy supplies in order to get the work accomplished. Recovery then takes place and some of the energy stores are replaced quickly so that you have enough energy to continue functioning the rest of the day.

The main recovery phase, however, takes place when you are sleeping. It is at this time that the body goes to work not only to repair any damage done to the muscles and tissues, but also to restructure them in response to the playing or training exercises completed. There is replenishment of the glycogen which restores your energy levels, and many other body functions take place to return your body to a stable state. Recovery and the changes that occur, however, are determined by the nutrients available in your body.

The body does not just compensate for what you have done or merely replace the energy supply that your body originally had. Your body undergoes specific structural and functional changes and deposits additional energy stores so that the next time you perform this amount of work it will be "easy" and you will be able to accomplish even more work. This is known as supercompensation. But if you do not go beyond your present level, your body will never get to the point of bringing about supercompensation. You will merely be recovering and maintaining yourself on the same level.

If you want to increase your capabilities, you have to exert yourself more than usual to get supercompensation. It is your ticket to progress, not only in your playing but also in your physical development. For supercompensation to occur, however, your body must have the needed nutrients to make the positive changes possible!

The following are brief discussions of the various facets of nutrition with which you should be familiar.

Fats

Fat is calorically denser than protein or carbohydrates. A single gram contains nine calories, while a gram of protein or carbohydrate contains about four. This is why the breakdown of fats provides double the energy of carbohydrates or protein. Diets high in saturated fat and transfats, however, are a risk factor for obesity, heart disease, high blood pressure, stroke, diabetes, and even some forms of cancer. A high-fat diet of mostly saturated fats typically leaves you feeling sluggish, so that you will not be able to play or exercise at your best. Thus, they should be avoided.

Good fats (mono- and polyunsaturated) must never be eliminated or severely cut back from the diet if you want to play a full game at your best. The body needs fat for many functions, which include assimilating fat-soluble vitamins and manufacturing essential enzymes and hormones. It is needed for recovery after severe workouts and for muscle hypertrophy. Fat also helps make food more satisfying and filling and it supplies the best energy for continuous playing.

Limit your intake of dietary fat to about 25-30 percent of your daily caloric intake. Start simply by cutting down on the most obvious foods that contain saturated fats, such as fried foods, rich sauces, hamburgers, hot dogs, full-fat salad dressings, mayonnaise and rich desserts. Use good oils, such as olive, canola, peanut, safflower, flaxseed or walnut, and be very selective in your use of other fats.

An excellent source of good fats is a snack of raw nuts. Use butter instead of margarine. Even though the virtues of margarine have been extolled for many years, we now know that it results in many more negative effects than does butter. Butter is a natural product the body can assimilate, while margarine, a transfatty acid, acts the same as a saturated fat and remains in your body for extended periods of time. Eat plenty of fish and fish oils, especially if you have a tendency to overdo the saturated fats. The fish oils will help move the saturated fats out of the body.

Proteins

Protein is needed to provide the basic building blocks for cellular muscular repair and development and to provide energy. While carbohydrates and fats supply most of the energy for muscular exertion, protein enables your muscles to respond to this exertion by getting stronger. Proteins also supply the brain with energy! This is why your need for protein increases the more you train the

Figure 17.2: Meats

muscles and involve the brain. Exercise causes the muscles to undergo a type of intricate cellular breakdown that only proteins can repair and build upon.

Figure 17.3: Fruits

Strength and speed-strength types of sports require greater amounts of protein (up to one gram per pound of weight) than other sports such as endurance sports. But even endurance events require ample protein for recovery and repair. An increase in protein dictates a decrease in carbohydrates. In this way, the extra protein allows for the creation of optimal conditions for maintaining and increasing your work capacity.

Your ability to recover is only possible with a definite combination of training loads and protein-rich foods. In addition to the protein, in order to start the optimal synthesis which provides tissue restoration and muscle hypertrophy and strength, you must have a sufficient amount of vitamins and lipids (fats). If you have a deficiency of vitamins, especially if you don't eat ample amounts of fresh fruits and vegetables, it can seriously interfere with the protein synthesis. In this case, it is strongly recommended that you supplement your diet with natural, whole-food vitamin/mineral supplements.

To get ample amounts of protein, you should eat mostly lean meats that contain your full complement of amino acids with less saturated fat. Concentrate on foods rich in high-quality protein, such as lean meats, poultry, eggs, beans and fish. Fresh raw nuts and seeds are also an excellent source of protein, fiber, vitamins and minerals.

Figure 17.4: Eggs

Regarding eggs — they are great foods and are not the culprit of increased cholesterol levels. The real culprit is the chicken feed! The feed is devoid of products such as lecithin, the key to breaking up cholesterol and moving it through the body. Natural or fertile eggs from cage-free chickens or from chickens fed a vegetable diet will not give you higher levels of cholesterol and are an excellent food.

Carbohydrates

Carbohydrates are great for fast energy and in some ways the most healthful type of food you can eat. This includes foods such as cereals, breads, potatoes, rice, beans, fruits and vegetables. Carbohydrates should be eaten in their natural, com-

Figure 17.5: Pasta

plex forms. Potato chips and candy bars don't count!

The more energy you have, the more inclined and the more capable you will be to have high-quality playing time and workouts. Some carbohydrates are unique; they rev up your body's metabolic rate, even when you're just resting or beginning to exercise, but only for a relatively short duration. If you play and work out for an hour or more, then fats (and some of the amino acids) become most important. The higher the intensity and duration of the workout, the more you will need to rely on fats.

When you play for long periods of time, in tournaments or practices, you will need an increased amount of carbohydrates as well as other nutrients. The key is not to use more carbohydrates during play but to have enough carbohydrates available for quick bursts of speed and explosive power when needed. Execution of quick bursts of speed and power rely on the anaerobic (without oxygen) processes. The fuel for this comes from your carbohydrates or sugars, which are used up quickly. Because of this, you must conserve them as much as possible so you will have an ample amount to last you through the time you will be playing.

However, there are exceptions to the use of carbohydrates. It seems that rather than being used up immediately for energy, carbohydrates in many women (and some men) are not immediately burned. They have the opposite effect; they make you tired and sluggish. Some doctors believe that carbohydrates tend to put on more weight with women, rather than being used for energy. Thus, it is important that you closely examine the effects that eating carbohydrates have on your body.

To fulfill your quota of valuable complex carbohydrates, which take longer to break down than the sugars, think beyond the popular white rice and white flour baked goods that have most of the nutrients removed. Choose from whole grain products and go for variety. Cornbread, muffins and pancakes made with whole grains and little fat are fine. Read the labels on pastries, taco shells, and pancake mixes for fat content. And stay away from corn chips (except blue corn chips), donuts, potato chips, high-fat crackers, cookies, cakes and sweet rolls. Many of these products contain sugar, a simple carbohydrate that is burned very quickly by the body to give you a "high", but which does not last very long.

Eating Hints

Vegetables should be a mainstay of your diet. When you make a salad, think beyond iceberg lettuce, which is practically void of any nutritional value. Use two or three different kinds of greens, such as spinach, red lettuce, chicory, escarole or romaine. Add items such as tomatoes, cucumbers, celery, green, yellow or red peppers, red or green onions, broccoli, cauliflower, carrots or any raw vegetable you enjoy. To further liven up salads, work in some foods from the grains and legumes groups and toss some peas or beans on your greens. Such salads can often be eaten without any dressing, which is usually loaded with bad fats. A little olive or canola oil, lemon juice and salt and pepper usually work wonders for additional taste.

Broccoli, carrots, zucchini, cauliflower, asparagus, green or red peppers, pea pods, green beans, chickpeas, mushrooms, turnips and tomatoes are great for snacks. These and other vegetables are very important for getting your vitamins and minerals and for keeping your body systems functioning well.

Figure 17.6: Salad

Fresh fruit is a reliable source of fiber and various vitamins and minerals. Choose whole fruit, preferably locally grown and naturally ripened, since it is more satisfying and nutritious. Fruit in season is more likely to be fresh. Carefully check out-of-season fruit to be sure it has not gone bad even if it looks good. For example, look for mold or fungus at the ends and smell for spoilage. Improvements in preserving fruits such as apples make it not uncommon to find some in the market that are over a year old! Because of this, you should not restrict yourself to only a few fruits. Learn to enjoy many different kinds!

Fat-Free Foods

Figure 17.7: Carrots

The number of low-fat and fat-free foods has increased astronomically over the past few years. However, studies show that people now eat more fat than they did before, and are still gaining weight because they are eating more. Thus, the culprit may not be simply high-fat foods: it may be adulterated foods! Best is to eat foods with the fat in its natural state and to not overeat. Avoid processed foods as much as possible. This is not easy, as it is rare to find pure unadulterated food in the markets!

Another drawback to eating low-fat and no-fat foods is that the reconstituted versions of the real thing lack fat-soluble nutrients and possibly other unknown nutrients. Scientists are still discovering new vitamins and minerals that up until now were not thought to be important to human health. To be sure you are getting an adequate supply of everything you need, your diet should include foods that are as close as possible to their natural state. Also, you should learn to substitute good oils for bad fats. For example, put olive oil on your bread instead of butter.

Don't rely on artificial sweeteners. Studies have found that over the course of a year, people who use artificial sweeteners are more likely to gain weight than non-users. The artificial sweeteners may increase feelings of hunger, since the brain interprets all sweeteners equally and triggers changes in blood sugar that mimic a reaction to sugar.

Keep It Simple

When it comes to preparing food, less is better. Don't overcook vegetables or obliterate otherwise healthy foods with high-fat cooking techniques, such as deep-frying or sautéing in gobs of lard or butter. It has been my experience that foods that are as close as possible to their natural state provide maximum nutrition and taste with minimum fuss. Try to appreciate foods for what they are, as opposed to what they become once adulterated by some high-fat garnish or sauce, and you will be that much ahead of the game.

No Meal Skipping

If you are a serious athlete, you should eat at least three to five times a day. That's right, no meal skipping and especially no fasting allowed. Your body is a finely tuned machine that needs fuel (nutrition) on a regular basis. The next time you are feeling too busy to eat and don't have time for a conventional meal, there is nothing wrong with a healthful snack, such as a piece of fruit, a small sandwich or some nuts. You will find that eating five to six mini-meals gives you more energy during the day.

The use of whole-food bars such as the Standardbars that contain a balance of various nutrients, vitamins and minerals are also beneficial, especially when there is insufficient time for a full meal to digest before a heavy practice or competition. However, beware of the food (energy) bars made from synthetic chemicals. They do not have the wholesome food benefits found in whole-food bars, and because of the sugar and other ingredients may even have negative effects.

Figure 17.8: Bottled water

Drink Lots of Water

As you probably know, water is extremely important for all athletes. It not only keeps you hydrated enough to play and exercise with maximum efficiency, but it also helps your body cool itself, eliminate its natural waste products and cleanse the pores. When you exercise you lose water, not just through sweat but also through your breathing, and the loss can be substantial. Nonetheless, you should use sparingly deodorants that block sweating and not use them at all during workouts or play as they can interfere with your body heat regulation and allow toxins to accumulate.

Perspiration depletes the body of water that must be replaced, so play it safe. Drink at least 10 to 15 eight-ounce glasses of water a day, which does not include soda, Gatorade, beer, coffee or tea. On hot days, increase the amount accordingly. And don't wait till you're thirsty to drink: your body can be short of water without your thirst letting you know about it.

According to Dr. Tobin Watkinson and other nutritionists, the only liquid that can totally rehydrate the cells is water. You can survive on colas, soft drinks, iced tea, or sparkling mineral waters, but they will not rehydrate the cells as water will. Water is the universal solvent. It enters the cell, rehydrates it and carries the waste materials away. You will not get these results with other drinks. The reason for this is that the pH in most drinks is inappropriate for the body. For example, a carbonated drink is acid, versus being alkaline, which is the normal environment to rehydrate the cell.

There are now many designer waters which are touted as rehydration drinks, including Gatorade. The unfortunate thing about these drinks is that they only contain one or two electrolytes and their major ingredient is some form of sugar. It may taste good at the moment, but you will not be feeling very well 20 minutes to an hour later. At this time you may be needing more nutrients or you will lose your concentration. Best is to have water that is not loaded with chemicals but contains minerals such as calcium, magnesium, potassium, sodium and others, as found in natural sea salt such as Celtic Salt.

Rehydration is especially important to active players, who should drink plenty of water every day. Keep in mind that your body is about 80-85 percent water, and you need to have a continuous supply of good water. Sadly, most of our regular tap water is basically a chemical bath: it is no longer natural water. For example, to naturally attract free-radical-like compounds in the body, the oxidation reduction potential (ORP) should be low.

In some major cities, such as San Diego, the ORP is 700-800 . Trinity Water from Idaho has an ORP of 50-75. And some artesian waters from New Zealand have an ORP of about 30-40. From my experiences and knowledge, the best drinking water is specially filtered tap water that has an ORP of -200 to -300. It is a very effective antioxidant and neutralizer of acidic conditions. The special filter is a combination of several different filters which get rid of chemicals and germs, add stable oxygen, make the water more alkaline and ionize and cluster the water for better absorption. For more information, visit www.lessacid.com.

Because of the sweating that you undergo in practice and in play, be sure you maintain your mineral levels, especially sodium. For this to happen, the water must have high mineralization, not low mineralization, as found in distilled and reverse-osmosis water. According to Dr. Watkinson the minerals should make the water slightly alkaline (pH of 8.5-9.5). Alkaline reserves are needed to neutralize acid build-up in the body not only from workouts, but also from the foods we eat such as meats, grains, sugar and alcohol. This acid build up is believed to be a major factor in causing many diseases.

In regard to fluid and electrolyte requirements, young athletes produce more metabolic heat per unit of body mass than do adults. This occurs mainly because of the increase in energy expenditure. For this reason, it is important that the extra heat generated be dissipated through sweat or you may induce heat-related illness. With excessive sweating, there is a possibility of greater loss of some electrolytes such as sodium. These are easily replaced at half-time or after the game by adding some minute amounts of natural sea salt to the water and the food.

Most important at this time is drinking sufficient amounts of water, especially good, clean water that is not loaded with chemicals. Note that a lack of water can limit playing ability much more than any loss of electrolytes! Understand that the energy your body needs is produced by the mitochondria, which operate like tiny engines inside the cells. In order to function properly, the mitochondria require a plentiful supply of water, electrolytes and nutrients.

When the cells can't exchange their debris-laden fluids for fresh, nutrient-rich fluids to keep the engines running, the cells will be unable to burn stored fat for energy. As a result, you will crave foods that are high in sugars and starches. This can lead to your body storing more fat.

Trained athletes, when acclimated to heat, produce much more sweat than non-athletes. Because of this, their fluid replacement requirements are considerably higher, which calls for drinking more water. Since

Figure 17.9: Drink lots of water

flavor of the drinking water is important, be sure that it is good, clean water which has a good taste. In many areas, tap water does not taste very good because of all the added chemicals, and you will not drink much.

One way to determine if you are getting enough water is to weigh yourself before and after a training session or after a major game. When there are major changes in body weight, it is usually due to loss of body fluid content. If you do not drink enough water to restore your normal body weight between practices or competitions, it will show up in the weighing. This will indicate the need for more water. However, do not rely only on this method to replace your water supply.

Cooling a drink may make water more palatable, but there are varying opinions as to how cold consumed water should be, especially when the body is hot. I typically recommend drinking water that is cool, but not cold. Hot water does not taste good, therefore, cooling is necessary. But when water is too cold, it is very hard to drink sufficient amounts and the extreme cold can shock the body unfavorably. Therefore, cool water appears to be the best. Adding a small amount of natural sea salt to the water, but not so much that the water tastes salty, will further stimulate your thirst and increase the amount of fluid that you can take in.

There are also some good waters on the market, such as Scientific Water Systems and some bottled artesian waters, that can help you recover after a workout. Some have oxygen added and contain no other additives or chemicals, making them an ideal supplement for recovery. Many players feel that this type of water makes the playing easier because of the resultant greater oxygen saturation in the blood.

They also experience faster recovery between halves and after games. For example, studies have shown that not only does OxyWater® have a positive physiological effect but also a noticeable performance effect, as athletes demonstrated after drinking it. By using such waters, you help your recovery and improve your performance at the same time.

Water is by far the best drink for rehydration. Carbohydrates do not rehydrate you. Because of this you should not confuse drinks that have carbohydrates and proteins added to them with rehydration drinks. They are not the same.

Eat Foods, Not Pills

I cannot overemphasize the importance of eating fresh and natural foods whenever possible. Don't let yourself be duped by the fantastic advertising claims often made for certain high-priced foods or supplements that are processed or synthetic. If you eat wisely and eat a variety of foods from the different categories, you shouldn't need many additional supplements. Supplementation, as the term implies, means to supplement your diet.

If you find your diet is lacking or your food is harvested from land that is depleted of nutrients, or if there are environmental conditions that lower the value of foods, then supplementation becomes very important. When you take supplements, be sure they are full, natural complexes of the various vitamins and minerals. In nature, vitamins and minerals are combined in varying degrees and should be eaten in their natural forms so that the body can better assimilate them and benefit from them. Synthetic products may create vitamin deficits in the body and not give you what your body truly needs.

For example, the synthetic version of vitamin C consists solely of ascorbic acid. But ascorbic acid is only one component of the total vitamin C complex. In addition to ascorbic acid, the natural vitamin C complex contains other vitamins and minerals to make it

Figure 17.10: Youngsters at play

complete. When you take only ascorbic acid, it robs the body of other nutrients in order to become complete and, if continued over a long period of time, can deplete you of other vitamins and minerals.

Enjoy Your Food

With a little imagination and not a lot of work, you can make your healthy diet extremely enjoyable. If your diet isn't giving you pleasure, it must be lacking in some aspects, regardless of how nutritionally complete it may be. Important, too, is allowing yourself some of your favorite foods, because many foods that you crave are trying to tell you something about your body's chemistry. A craving for something sweet, for example, could be a sign that your blood sugar has fallen too low. (Don't make this a habit though.) Or a strong urge for something salty could mean the sweat you are losing in your workouts has caused your body's sodium levels to dip. Use natural sea salt, such as Celtic Salt, to make up for any loss and to get a full complement of minerals.

Learn to respect your body's messages if you are serious about your sport and your health, because they are usually telling you something you should know. If you are working out regularly, the food you eat will have a purpose. The more you compete and train, the more you should find yourself migrating to better and healthier foods, mainly because you will see the difference in how you play and how you feel.

Carbohydrates or Fats for Energy?

As you start to exercise or play, your energy levels are usually high. You utilize a fair amount of the sugars (carbohydrates) that are present in your body from the stores of glycogen. Once you have depleted these, your body turns to burning fats which produce much more energy. As a result you usually see a difference between the beginning, middle and end of play with respect to how you play as well as how you feel.

However, if you limit the amount of fat you include in your diet and replenish the carbohydrate stores by constantly ingesting carbohydrate foods and carbohydrate-type drinks during the workout or during play, your body will limit the burning of fats. As a result, you will not be able to utilize the fats in the body. This is a very inefficient use of energy.

Fats are not automatically burned effectively. You must train your body to burn fats for high energy, especially in the endurance events. One of the most effective regimes for doing this is to work out close to your anaerobic threshold and to sustain it for as long as possible. In competitive team sports, you play in high anaerobic ranges intermittently. But, if you are trained to use fats efficiently, you will rely more on fats in recovery and then be able to perform longer and with top efficiency.

Elite speed-strength (power) athletes have their heart rate around 160-200 beats per minute (BPM) for the entire game. Because of this, it is impossible to replenish the amount of carbohydrates necessary to continuously play in this high zone. The more carbohydrates you use up in your reserves, the less you will have for finishing the game well or at a fast pace.

Keep in mind that when you start feeling tired, it is not necessarily because of cardiovascular or respiratory system fatigue; it may be due to your lack of fuel to continue. In this case, it is most likely the fact that you have used up your carbohydrate reserves and are now unable to rely on your fat reserves. The key to playing on a high level is to get your body to the point where it can burn fat more efficiently as the intensity of the work increases, and reserve the carbohydrates for the highest intensity levels.

The fact that the body relies greatly on fats to fuel your overall playing over the course of a game is so obvious that it has been greatly overlooked. Fitness literature recognizes that if you wish to lose fat you must work out longer and at a faster pace. As a result, your body utilizes more fat for energy and you lose the fat stores. But I am always amazed at the diets often recommended for athletes that contain mostly carbohydrates, which delay the burning of fats.

For example, recent studies have substantiated that fat is the predominant energy source during prolonged exercise, such as in endurance races, soccer, lacrosse, field hockey, volleyball and other speed-strength sports. Also, children use relatively more fat and less carbohydrates than adolescents or adults. This is the reason adults should not superimpose adult eating habits on youngsters. During short, intense runs, children rely more on aerobic energy metabolism in which fat is the major energy source. They do not rely on the anaerobic energy metabolism as do teenagers and adults. This is a distinct difference between very young children and older seasoned players.

Many players who carbo-load or who have high carbohydrate stores at the beginning of play cannot complete a full game going all-out or play well in the second half or in overtime — they literally run out of gas. The body is unable to utilize more fats and it may not have a sufficient amount of fat for it to use. Understand that the body will maintain a minimal amount of fat and cannibalize the muscles before it will use up all the fat in the body.

Because of this, I seriously question the practice of maintaining an extremely high carbohydrate diet or using carbohydrate drinks before playing and during time-outs. If you eat a more balanced diet and train your body to utilize fats, you may find that your playing (and workout) efficiency improves tremendously.

Your energy comes from your nutrition which your body uses in different ways. For simplicity, think of energy production as coming from three different assembly lines: fats, carbohydrates and proteins. Each assembly line is capable of producing energy. The amount of material on the assembly line moving toward the final product depends upon a number of different reactions that occur along the way. Think of these reactions as gates preventing or interfering with the flow of the nutritional material.

The simplest assembly line is the sugar (carbohydrate) line which has few to no gates along the way. Thus, the sugar will pass without interruption and quickly create energy at the end. However, the amount of material available on the sugar assembly line is quite variable. You can receive an immediate flood of material followed by no or very little material. This scene can be repeated indefinitely unless the foodstuffs that are being put into the assembly line are complex carbohydrates. Complex carbohydrates require more digestion, producing a lower but more consistent flow of foodstuffs and more consistent production of energy.

Fats and proteins require many intermediate steps and require multiple cofactors, vitamins, minerals and other chemical reactions to move through the gates in order to maintain a constant flow to produce energy. If the items that operate the gates are not available, the energy resulting from either protein or fat breakdown will be disrupted.

Thus, the digestion of fats and proteins relies on the availability of needed nutrients to supply energy. Yet sugars, especially when in a processed form (such as white sugar), require so little digestion (few gates) that they can maintain an energy source as long as a continuous supply of the foods containing processed carbohydrates is available.

Examples of athletes who get their energy this way are those who go from one sugared cup of coffee to the next, or one sugar-covered doughnut to the next or one carbohydrate sports drink or energy bar to the next. In this case, you're basically supplying your energy needs by simple processed sugars.

What many athletes do not realize is that fats and proteins are essential, and without these ingredients you have no long-lasting sources of energy that are especially critical for endurance athletes. Nor do you have the foodstuffs or material necessary for proper brain chemistry (brain functioning, especially thinking and decision-making), muscular development, hormone production and operation, organ repair and many more.

Proteins are the result of an accumulation of individual building blocks called amino acids of which there are many. Eight amino acids are considered essential, which means that you cannot exist without them. With these eight amino acids your body can make the rest of the amino acids that you need. It is only recently that scientists have looked closely at the role of protein and are discovering how important it is not only for performance but also for energy production, repair and how it works synergistically with carbohydrates and fats.

The bottom line is that if you want constant, steady production of energy, you must have ample amounts of fats in the diet. Understand that fats are not bad. Saturated fats can be bad if eaten in large quantities. But the polyunsaturated and monounsaturated fats are great for the body and are an excellent source of energy production. Thus, do not skimp on eating foods that have substantial amounts of fat.

Adjust Your Eating

According to Dr. Watkinson, energy expenditure and nourishment for players depends to a large extent on the demands of the workout or competition.

Time your meals so that if you are a morning person, you have your heavier starch, protein and vegetables for breakfast. An omelet would be an excellent choice. The midmorning snack should include nuts and seeds, proteins which keep your sugars up but don't give you an overabundance. They will run your brain very well. It is best to have raw and unsalted nuts, unless you play in very hot weather, in which case adding a little natural sea salt is good. In addition, eat the nuts and seeds by themselves since they can be digested more easily and efficiently on an empty stomach. When nuts and seeds get cooked (roasted) they can go bad.

If you are an afternoon or evening person and play in the morning, you should start your day with fruit and have a midmorning snack of a more substantial protein such as beef jerky. Evening persons need to have the fruits in the morning to raise their blood sugar. If you have some fruit and then a vegetable snack later, you will do better.

For an afternoon game, the lunch for a morning and afternoon person is basically the same. At lunch do not choose only one food item such as pasta or a sandwich. If you eat too much protein at lunch, you'll get tired in the afternoon and you'll soon find yourself yawning. Too much starch or protein will be converted to sugars, making them inappropriate for lunch as well. An ideal lunch would include lots of vegetables and a little protein such as fish or chicken with some carbohydrates. A morning person should have starch in the morning, and a night person should have starch at night.

Drinking soft drinks or alcohol can be detrimental when working out or playing. The alcohol will dehydrate you and affect your blood sugar, as will soft drinks and sodas. Any of the sugary soft drinks and fruit juices which you might think would be great are, in fact, not very good. Eating the whole fruit is much better than just having the juice, which often has added water or other juices and in some cases, artificial preservatives. Read the labels carefully and you will find that many fruit drinks do not contain any fruit juice! If you drink cola beverages, you are more susceptible to fractures than those who don't, and you usually don't eat enough green vegetables to get ample calcium in your diet. This increases your risk for thin, fragile bones that break more easily.

If you are a morning person you should have a snack of some fruit in the afternoon. If you are a night person, you should have the nuts in the middle of the afternoon that the morning person had in the middle of their morning. You need the protein to make it through to your dinner!

After a game or practice, compensate for your energy loss by consuming ample amounts of food. The protein, fats, carbohydrates, and minerals received from food are in a very complex and multicomponent chemical system. The body receives more than 80 different food substances, including essential nonsynthesized food factors, such as indisposable amino acids, indisposable polyunsaturated fatty acids, vitamins and minerals. From these nutrients, the body synthesizes tens of thousands of necessary substances in various combinations for not only the life activity of the body but also for playing sports.

The problem you face is determining which essential food substances are the most important. A deficiency of one of these nutrients can lead to insufficient production of hundreds of combinations which are necessary for you, and even a surplus of merely one nutrient can interfere with the balance of others. All serious athletes should receive the necessary balance of nutrients from a wide assortment of products. The approximate amounts of the daily requirement for athletes (which have not been determined) vary according to the different sports.

Young athletes are often faced with two nutritional challenges: inadequate energy intake and a nutritionally unbalanced diet. These are the areas in need of great improvement, and will affect your playing ability quite dramatically. If your diet is properly composed and meets the energy needs encountered in game play, you will not only have a greater physical work capacity, but you will also be able to recover faster. Recovery is most important as it then enables you to practice or compete well on the same day or when you have multiple games. Studies have shown that players are able to increase their work capacity by 20 percent when their diets are balanced, optimally composed, and high in energy.

Figure 17.11: Nuts

Keep in mind that you are not like your nonathletic peers. How your body handles the various nutrients and foods you eat is different from relatively inactive people. For example, if you consume excess amounts of calcium, sodium, magnesium and phosphorus, it will not increase your physical work capacity. But when these minerals are taken together in a complex, there is a strong beneficial effect, especially concerning the maximum amount of oxygen that you can utilize during play. Nonathletes do not exhibit this correlation.

Maintaining Concentration

According to Dr. Watkinson, athletes need to maintain their concentration throughout, and especially near the end of, a game. Concentration is basically brain chemistry — a balance between your ability to utilize the fuel that you have taken in and your ability to convert it into the appropriate brain chemistries. All the amino acids, which are the small building blocks of proteins, are the precursors to building the brain chemistries we hear so much about today. This includes serotonin, melatonin, epinephrine, and norepinephrine, as well as other substances that our brains need to function well.

If you are exercising or playing under stress, you are going to use a higher amount of your brain fuels. If you are unable to replenish these fuels because you have burned up the raw material or have inadequate food nutrients, your body will stall. If you have a high demand for brain fuels, such as during an important competitive game, and your body is unable to have the appropriate fuels to do what is needed, you will be unable to concentrate.

Emotional needs require even more nutritional support. When there is a heavy emotional component (such as when you are playing in a league or championship game), you can burn up to 25 percent more calories than in regular play or practice! This is why it is so important to be well-fortified nutritionally. Keep in mind that the minimum standards established for various vitamins and minerals are for sedentary people, not athletes. You need more, in some cases many more, than the average person!

Conclusion

Be sure to eat a wide range of foods and to follow the guidelines that have been discussed. This means having ample amounts of vegetables, meats, breads, nuts, legumes, seeds and fruits in order to benefit from the full range of these very rich sources of all vitamins and minerals. Unfortunately, many people today are taking synthetic and incomplete vitamins that create vitamin deficiencies which cause some of the mental "fogs" that people get into at times. We are not as smart as nature in our ability to produce a nutrient that is as complete as what nature can produce.

NOTES:

Chapter 18
Performance-Enhancing Drugs

This book would not be complete without discussing the use of drugs in sport. According to published and unpublished reports, it now appears that a considerable number of American athletes use drugs in order to improve their performance. You can find many examples of drug use in high school (and sometimes before) through the professional levels. The athletes who use drugs, mainly steroids, believe the drugs make them better athletes. This could not be further from the truth.

If you follow the program and guidelines presented in this book, there is no need for drugs. There is no questioning the fact that drugs are effective and can help you in various ways. Steroids help build more muscle, and stimulants such as caffeine and "uppers" can help you perform above and beyond your usual capabilities. The use of EPO and other drugs enables you to go longer and farther in endurance events.

In all cases, however, the price for using drugs is very high, ranging from personality changes such as "roid rage," to various physical problems. But it appears that some athletes are willing to take the risk even when they know it can kill them. This is a sad but true statement that shows how strongly athletes believe they need drugs in order to be successful.

This belief comes from their peers and some successful professional athletes. The original idea most likely came from the media reporting on the East German and Soviet athletes in the 1970s and 80s, many of whom were the best in the world. The media repeatedly emphasized that these athletes had to be using drugs in order to be so successful. The United States was by no means clean at that time, as many athletes were also using drugs, but the overpowering media bombardment on alleged drug use by the Soviets, East Germans and other East Bloc countries became so firmly entrenched that almost everyone believed these athletes won only because of drugs.

Overlooked in all this slanted reporting was the nature of these athletes' training regimens. Their programs were the most sophisticated and successful ever seen in the world. Even now, we are still discovering different aspects of the training programs used by the Soviets and East Germans and incorporating them into the training of U.S. athletes.

For example, the concepts of periodization, cycling, specificity of training and plyometrics were all developed to the highest levels by these countries. Everything was based on science; very little was left to chance. These countries had some of the top physicists, exercise physiologists, doctors, psychologists, coaches, massage practitioners and others, all working together as a team to develop high-level athletes.

Understand that these foreign countries did not have large sports foundations. For example, the Soviet Union only had a few swimming pools in the entire country. The number of tennis courts could be counted on one or two hands. Gyms were found only in the schools. Consequently, they had to select athletes with the greatest potential and apply scientific principles to their training in order to develop their maximum potential as quickly as possible. They did not have hundreds of thousands of players to chose from, as is evident in the U.S. in sports such as basketball and track and field, where a few great athletes rise to the top simply from the laws of chance. The Soviets and East Germans meanwhile had to literally create the athlete. They were able to take raw talent and mold it into a high-level athlete.

In addition, these countries had to produce coaches who were capable of working with and improving youngsters as well as the highest-level athlete. To this end, they established coaching institutes that had extremely high standards. Before one could even apply to become a coach, he or she had to be a regional or national sports champion. They then had to take a week of academic exams, and those who survived became students at the institutes. During this time, they still continued their athletic training for a third or half of each day; the rest of the day was spent on academics.

I visited these institutes and was very impressed. For example, in the track-and-field departments, they had films on every top performer in the world. In addition, the scientists had the performances and training programs analyzed, highlighting strong and weak points. Based on what the world's best athletes were doing, they then improved upon the technique and methods of training to make their athletes more successful. Those institutes were able to develop coaches who understood all of the nuances of the sport. When these high-level and well-educated athletes became coaches, they then had major responsibilities working with the better athletes since there were no mass programs for the general population at that time.

The Soviets developed a training system that was extremely successful, one that we are only now beginning to incorporate gradually in the United States. Because of its success, many elements of their program are presented in this book. The concepts and training plans are based on practical use by the athletes, so they have a proven record. The guidelines are not merely theory but have been well-proven in practice. By following these recommendations, you can also experience great success.

If you rely on drugs, you may achieve success, but it will be short-lived, and you will be cheating yourself out of the potential you may have. Simply look at some of the baseball players who achieved great success for one or two years but then were unable to compete subsequently. When athletes started getting tested for steroids and other drugs, there

Figure 18.1: Football

was a noticeable decrease in the size and corresponding performance of many players. This shows that they relied on the steroids and not on their training to make them better.

Players who use steroids often forget that the effect of these drugs is highly individualized. One person might use large doses safely for many years without suffering apparent harm, while another might develop cancer. In addition, a particular drug may be very effective for one athlete, but useless for another. When you use the same steroid for long periods, it may lose its effectiveness unless the dosage is increased to possibly hazardous levels. This is why it is not uncommon to find some athletes using two or three different steroids every day for three or four months. Last, but certainly not least, is the fact that the cost of steroids is high, sometimes thousands of dollars each year.

By using drugs and believing that drugs improve your performance, you do not train harder to develop your full potential. You become lazy, or overtrain for some physical qualities, especially strength where drugs have their greatest effect. You rely on the drugs to improve your performance rather than using time-tested and proven methods as outlined in this book. When you use a scientifically based approach, there is little need for drugs. You will find yourself making progress equal to if not better than someone who is using drugs. I guarantee this!

When you train scientifically, you develop many skills and abilities—not just one or two physical abilities that drugs allow you to develop well. As a result, you become much better at many different aspects of the game play. In essence, you become more athletic and a better overall athlete who can execute the skills and plays more effectively. Equally important is that you will have your physical abilities developed commensurate with your technique.

Understand that you do not need maximum strength or maximum endurance, especially when playing team sports. Maximum strength is important only in the strength sports such as weightlifting, where you must exhibit the greatest amount of strength. Maximum muscular and cardiorespiratory endurance is only needed in endurance events such as the marathon, where you must demonstrate the greatest amount of endurance.

All team sports require combinations of qualities, not maximum development of any one. In baseball, developing maximum strength may allow you to hit the ball further but not become a better runner or fielder. You need optimal amounts of specific physical qualities based on your technique. Thus, if you train as outlined in this book and in some of the recommended books, you will achieve more success than by simply using drugs to become better in one physical quality, which can then impede the development of your other physical qualities.

Use of effective nutrition and restorative measures are other ways to duplicate the effects of drugs. For example, it is not uncommon to find endurance athletes using steroids, not to build muscle but rather to aid in recovery. The steroids allow you to recover faster, so you can do more training.

Different restorative measures ranging from nutrition to the sauna to physical therapy, and physical methods such as electrical stimulation can achieve the same results without the negative effects. These methods are well-known but have not been put into athletic practice in the United States. Most training rooms have only whirlpools and sometimes a large jacuzzi. These are far from sufficient to provide adequate recovery for the athletes after intense training or game play. Most often this equipment is used in injury treatment rather than game recovery.

Nutrition plays a key role in recovery. Some whole-food (not synthetic!) vitamins and minerals can give you a boost similar to that produced by steroids. They replace the nutrients used up in your performance, enabling you to be ready sooner to train or play. The nutrients will also be used for greater supercompensation. When the vitamins and minerals are natural food products, there is no danger of them being classified as a drug. You must however, beware of synthetic versions of various supplements.

The effects from using drugs are not lasting. Once you lay off them, you will see an immediate decrease in your strength levels as well as in your performance. Thus, the benefits from using drugs are temporary, whereas the benefits from developing yourself through natural means are more permanent. Of course, if you completely lay off training, there will be some losses of strength and other physical qualities and abilities, but if you maintain your training on a year-round basis as outlined previously, the training effects will stay with you from year to year.

When you use drugs and have to go off them for a certain portion of the year to eliminate some of the negative effects, you will lose what strength and physical abilities you gained. When you start using drugs again, you will only attain the level achieved previously. Thus, you do not achieve the additional gains from year to year that you need to become a better athlete.

The key to success in training is to be able to recover quickly after a workout. This is a most valuable factor for improving your performance. Understand that the faster you can recover, the more training you can accomplish, and the greater will be the gains you can achieve. All of this can be achieved naturally; it does not require the use of drugs.

If you believe that drugs are the answer to your success, you will never fully achieve your potential greatness. This is also true of coaches who rely on drugs in their training. For example, I had a coach come to me with his athlete for analysis of his running technique and training program. After analyzing his performance, I made several key recommendations that would greatly improve his technique and physical abilities. We spent nearly three hours discussing his technique and training program, but as we were ending the meeting, the coach pulled me to the side and asked, "What are the main drugs used by the Soviets?" He had only wanted to find out what drugs he could use. Sadly, the athlete never developed his great potential and soon became a has-been. Don't let this happen to you.

NOTES:

Chapter 19
The Training Program

To understand the basics of a sound, scientifically based training program, it is necessary to look at the general concept of how an athlete should be nurtured from the very earliest years to his years as a professional. This is known as a multi-year training program, and it outlines what should take place over the years based on results from your training and playing.

In an annual training program, you follow the same progression of training phases each year, but the level, type and amount of training changes in accord with your abilities. Thus, even though the general concept of the training for each month of the year is the same, the exact work being done can be substantially different each year. A training program for a low-level athlete is of little benefit to a high-level athlete and vice versa.

The multi-year program has general guidelines to guide you over the years, but the annual program has specific workouts and routines within each year. The guidelines with specific recommendations must be adjusted for your sport and your abilities. For example, the amount of strength and type of strength needed in your sport at your level of play must be adjusted each year. As a result, the strength training can be substantially different for you and other athletes. See Chapter Two for information on the multi-year training program.

The Annual (Year-Round) Training Plan

To determine how your workouts should be distributed throughout the year, it is important to understand the concept of periodization and cycling. In periodization, your yearly plan (or semi-annual if you have major competition twice a year) is divided into different periods, or phases of training. In each phase you train in a specific manner to gain certain physical qualities or attain certain results. The development you achieve enables you then to undertake the training called for in the next period of training. Each phase of training leads to your ultimate goal.

The periods and the types of training vary for each athlete. Because most players have multiple objectives, the training must have several directions in order to concentrate on qualities such as technique, strength, flexibility, various aspects of speed-strength (explosive) and endurance training.

If you are on a year-round competitive schedule, it is extremely difficult to maintain an effective training program. When you are constantly competing, there is little time to prepare yourself for the best playing. Remember that playing is not an effective way to increase your strength, speed, quickness or other physical qualities.

Figure 19.1: Heel raises

Because of this, I recommend that you select a particular competitive period, match or competition that is most important, and then establish a training program around this event. This allows you to train through certain competitions or competitive periods so that they become training sessions. You still play your best, but it may not be as good as if you had trained specifically for that competition. This allows you to prepare yourself to play your best when the major season arrives.

Doing this is also effective for athletes who play two or more varsity sports. If the athletes are 15-16 years of age, they select their primary sports and train through the other sports. However, doing this is not effective when the athlete is 18 years or older. At this time they should have one primary sport. Younger athletes are encourged to play two or more sports.

Phase One: General Physical Preparation

The initial stage of training consists of general preparatory (general physical conditioning) exercises to strengthen all the major muscles and joints. Some specialized strength exercises are also included to prepare you better for the more intense training to follow. This period is also used for rehabilitation of injured muscles and joints and strengthening lagging muscles. The work in this period is general in nature so that psychological stress does not build. The volume of work done is high but the intensity is low.

Figure 19.2: Jump out of a squat

This is an introductory period which may also include low-level playing practice.

The exact length of time spent in this phase depends upon your mastery of the strength exercises and sport skills, your level of fitness, age, sex and so on. The younger or more novice you are, the more time you spend in this phase of training in order to adequately increase strength, endurance and other physical qualities. For beginners, this phase can last up to three or four months.

If you are a high-level player you may spend two to four weeks in this period, mainly to raise the body to a level that will enable you to start intense training. This is based on the assumption that you remain in good physical condition and that you have maintained your skills throughout the year. For most players, this period lasts approximately six to eight weeks.

The general all-around strength program includes many strength exercises. For the lower body, exercises include the heel raise, toe raise, squat, hip abduction and adduction, knee drive, hip extension

Cinematogram 19.1: Single-Leg Side Jump

Frame 1   Frame 2   Frame 3   Frame 4

Frame 5   Frame 6   Frame 7   Frame 8

(pawback), good morning, glute-ham-gastroc raise, knee curls and leg extensions. These lower-body exercises develop the leg and hip muscles in different actions, most of which are important in running, cutting and jumping.

Midsection exercises include the reverse sit-up, reverse trunk twist, 45-degree sit-up, back raise and back raise with a twist. These exercises play a very important role not only in strengthening the back to help prevent injury, but also in developing a muscular corset around the midsection. A strong midsection is needed to transfer the forces from the legs to the upper body in jumping and for powerful sprinting and cutting. Upper-body exercises can vary greatly but should include exercises for the chest, back and arms.

These strength exercises are beneficial since they use all of the major and many of the minor muscles involved in a multitude of movements. They prepare your body for more intense weight training

Cinematogram 19.2: Explosive Side Lunge

Frame 1   *Frame 2*   *Frame 3*

exercises and for executing sport skills more effectively. Some of these exercises can be used for rehabilitation purposes while others can be used to strengthen muscles that have been weakened because of a long lay-off or overuse in particular movements. As you work on general strength, you should also work to improve the technique of your sport skills.

Phase Two – Specialized Physical Training

The specialized physical training period begins gradually as the general preparatory period comes to an end. In specialized physical training, the work is very specific to the sport skills. This means practicing the specific game skills and doing specific exercises for increasing strength, speed-strength, endurance, etc., exactly as needed in competition. The exercises duplicate the same range of motion, type of muscular contraction and motor pathways seen in the execution of the game skills. As a result, the exercises enhance specific skill execution.

Your exact workout at this time depends upon your level of ability and stage of training. For example, a program to improve speed and cutting actions for a baseball, football, softball, basketball or tennis player might consist of the following exercises:

- Explosive side jumps
- Single-leg side, forward and backward jumps
- Explosive Lunge with Active Cords
- Explosive Side lunge with Active Cords

- Ankle abduction/adduction with Active Cords
- Knee extensions

For improved running speed and a quick first step:
- Jumps out of a squat
- Plyometric (explosive) exercises
- Quick (reactive) movements out of the athletic stance
- Lunge with Active Cords
- Knee drive with Active Cords
- Pawback with Active Cords
- Explosive ankle jumps

More advanced players may have a similar program, but it will usually include more sets of the explosive exercises or use a split program to perform lower body, midsection and total body explosive exercises together with specialized strength exercises. A sample program is outlined below.

Monday and Thursday

To improve cutting ability and running speed:
- Explosive single-leg and double-leg side jumps and jumps for height
- Split-squat jumps with weights in the hands or against the pull of rubber tubing
- Four-way floor jumps, single and double leg.
- Ankle jumps
- Explosive thigh drive

Each of these exercises is done for two-to-three sets of 10 repetitions.

These explosive exercises are then followed with lower-body strength exercises such as squats, heel raises, standing knee extensions, glute-ham-gastroc raises, back raises, hip extensions, hip abductions, lunges, ankle adduction/abduction with Active Cords.

Tuesday and Friday

- Push-up jumps
- Medicine ball throws (sidearm and overhead)
- Medicine ball catches and throws done explosively
- Push-press
- Traveling push-up jumps

These explosive exercises are then followed by special strength exercises such as the free motion presses, triceps press, triceps push-down, bench press, glute-ham sit-ups, Russian twist, back raises with a twist, front arm raises, standing cable row, lat pulldown, overhead pulldowns and overhead presses.

Wednesday and Saturday

On Wednesday and Saturday, specialty work is done for specific skills and physical abilities. The exact work depends on your objectives and specific needs. Most athletes should work on greater improvement of sports skills. To do this, integrate the training so that you can include all of the different types of training in a timely and effective manner. By the end of this period you should be ready to begin competition on a high level.

Phase Three – The Competitive Period

During the competitive period your training should be devoted to maintaining and/or improving some of the physical qualities already developed. In individual, team and dual sports, you should not be increasing strength at this time, as it will adversely affect your technique. In the competitive period, skill perfection and the ability to implement the skills during game play is paramount. You do not want to increase your physical abilities, except for speed and quickness in the execution of game-specific actions, because any strength increases will change your skill execution.

The main focus in the competitive period should be on the perfection of technique and the development of the psychological and strategic aspects of the game. They should be worked on together with the execution of the competitive game skills in practice, in scrimmages and in competitive game play. Keep in mind that your physical abilities have already been developed to their optimal levels during the specialized period of training. Further increases should not be needed!

Because the actual daily training workouts at this time depend to a great extent on your coach, no details are presented here. Suffice it to say that in practice you should be executing many plays and drills to enhance your play-making ability as well as your ability to carry out the strategies being developed. This is where your work on offense and defense becomes extremely important.

Phase Four – The Post-Competitive Period

After competition you should go through a stage of recuperation and relaxation, especially from a mental standpoint. At this time the body can still do physical work but the mind must rest. Active rest is best. This means that you remain active for relaxation purposes, not for physical development. At this time it is beneficial to participate in a different sport that you enjoy so you can still experience the physical work but gain enjoyment and satisfaction from the activity to help you relax. The better your skills and abilities in this secondary sport, the greater will be your relaxation and enjoyment.

The post-competitive period usually lasts two to four weeks, depending upon the length of your season and your wind-down period. This phase is very important and should not be omitted, regardless of whether you play for a few months or on a year-round basis.

If you played very little during the season, playing in the post-competitive period can be beneficial. It is at this time that you can put your game skills to the test and experience competitive play. You do not have to relax in the same manner as the athlete who played most of the games during the season.

If you find that you are relatively weak and need greater strength, you can immediately begin a specific training program. The more time you spend developing strength, the more easily you will be able to develop speed and explosiveness to prepare you to play on a par with higher-level players.

By using this plan, it is possible to achieve the highest levels of speed, power, skill — the keys to successful play in your sport. Each phase of training builds on the previous phase and results in your best performance during the competitive period. Equally important to ensure that you get the most out of each training phase is periodization of your nutrition. It is critical to eat and supplement your nutrition according to your training.

Cycling

Cycling means repeating the same movements or actions over a period of time, such as the leg action in running or squats in your training on certain days for specific numbers of repetitions. You repeat the exercise or workout for a few days, weeks or months until you achieve a training effect — until you experience physiological changes in the body from the training that you did.

If you change the training program every week, your body will not have sufficient time to attain the training effect. Understand that the body adapts to increases in strength and other abilities only when there is repetition of a particular stimulus for a certain amount of time. The stimulus in this case is the exercise or workout. You can add greater resistance for overload, but the exercises and number of sets and repetitions should remain basically the same.

After your body adapts to the workout program (you get a training effect) a change is needed. Otherwise, your body will rebel from the boredom of the same routine, and your muscle gains will cease and in some cases reverse. In essence, there is stagnation in the nervous system and the muscles are no longer stimulated to respond. This is a catch-22 situation. You must continue the exercise routines in the same way for a certain period of time to get the needed increases. But continuing the exercises or program for too long brings about negative changes. Thus, you must change the routine to get renewed energy of the nervous system and continued growth.

The key to success is knowing when to make the necessary changes to restimulate the nervous system. This is the secret to effective cycling, and is possible only if you maintain detailed diaries of your workouts. Most often you will see a leveling of results to signify full adaptation and indicate that a change is needed.

For example, high-level, well-conditioned players must change basic exercises such as the squat every three to five weeks in order to see constant gains. Beginners and intermediates, however, may continue to experience gains for up to three to four months! Thus there is a wide gap between different levels of performers. When other exercises are examined, even greater variability can be seen. Because of this, a differentiated approach is needed, geared to your level of fitness, exercise and sports mastery.

When cycling your workouts during the week (micro cycle), you must not have many consecutive days of very intense workouts. You should have an intense day followed by an easy or moderate one, and alternate in this manner over the week. When getting ready to peak (preparing for competition), it is possible to have two or three heavy days in a row followed by some lighter days. Also after every three weeks or so – especially if the workouts are fairly intense – you should have a relatively light to moderate workout week to allow your body more time for full adaptation and to help the body recover. Doing this prevents overtraining.

Perfecting Your Technique

To make your technique (skill) work most effectively, you should follow several very important guidelines:

(1) Always be energetic and alert when practicing. Understand that all skills are neuromuscular skills. They require the combined active involvement of the nervous system with the muscular system.

Figure 19.3: The knee drive

Thus, the nerves and muscles must have high energy levels in order to carry out the necessary movements with precision. This is the reason technique work is always done first in the training session or done separately at another time of day, when you are not feeling fatigued.

(2) Do not repeat one skill or a portion of a skill for excessively long periods of time. Perform the movement until you can no longer do it as well or in the same movement pattern. Stop at the first signs of fatigue so that you do not develop a different neuromuscular pathway for execution of the skill. You must learn the one most effective technique and reinforce it the same way until it becomes automatic. If you are well-trained, your body will automatically make the necessary changes when you are tired to ensure effective execution of the skill. Do not learn or practice skills when you are in a fatigued state!

(3) Keep your practice sessions relatively short. For example, when working on a cutting technique it is important that you concentrate on the movements being executed. After 20 to 30 repetitions you have probably accomplished as much as possible to making the necessary changes. Then switch to a different skill or joint action. Working on technique involves total mental concentration as well as full body energy in order to carry out the necessary actions.

(4) Follow the technique work with specialized strength exercises to reinforce more strongly the specific joint actions. For example, when working on the knee drive action to improve the quickness of your first step or running speed, do the knee drive strength exercise in the same way on every repetition to reinforce the feel of driving the knee forward. Visualize the action. In this way you can enhance the technique execution and gain additional strength. Execution of a special strength exercise takes maximum concentration to develop the correct movement pathway and muscle feel to duplicate the same action every time during play.

Perfecting Your Physical Abilities

When first starting a specialized strength exercise, do one exercise for three to five repetitions with light resistance. When using rubber tubing, adjust the length so that you can execute the exercise easily through a full ROM. Execute each repetition at a moderate rate of speed.

As you perform the exercise, concentrate on the technique and how it feels. Recognize which muscles are working in each exercise. In this way you will gain a better feel for the movement and how it relates to specific abilities. After completing three to five repetitions, relax before preparing for the next exercise. Proceed in this manner until you complete all the exercises selected.

Do the set of exercises for two to six weeks, especially when learning them. Record each exercise and the number of repetitions completed so that you know exactly how to proceed at the next workout and to note your progress.

When to Work Out

Schedule your main workouts so that they do not fall immediately before or after practice or play. An ideal situation would be to schedule strength and other exercises in the morning and to play (or practice) in the afternoon. If you prefer playing in the morning, you should do the exercises in the late afternoon or evening. The key here is to give yourself a few hours of rest and recovery in between. Do the exercises consistently and at a fairly regular time so that you have ample time to recover and to adapt to the exercises. When there is insufficient time, limit yourself to general strength exercises after practice.

Repetitions and Sets

When first beginning, add one or two repetitions to the strength exercises at each workout (or each week) until you reach 15 to 20 repetitions maximum (RM). This means you cannot do any more repetitions with the resistance selected. When you repeatedly reach 20 RM (or slightly more) you will be ready to increase the resistance for that particular exercise.

After a few weeks you will become more comfortable with the exercises and have greater confidence. Since you will be able to handle more resistance and execute more repetitions without any discomfort or trepidation, you can add other exercises at this time. If you experience soreness on any workout day or on the following day, it means you did too many repetitions or used too much resistance. When this happens, use less resistance in the next workout to help your body recover. Gradually increase the resistance or repetitions as you feel up to it. To aid in your recovery and to help prevent soreness, many players have found the use of supplements such as Velvet Antler to be effective.

Figure 19.4: Velvet Antler

Do only one set of each exercise. A set is a particular number of repetitions of one exercise one time. For example, if you do 20RM of the squat, this constitutes one set of the exercise. If you then do an additional 20 RM or less, it is considered a second set.

The main purpose of the workout program at this time is to familiarize you with the exercises and to have your body adapt gradually to the workout. Doing more than one set will not produce greater increases in strength. A greater number of sets is needed only when you require greater gains after you become more fit and have better mastery of the exercises. Additional sets play their most important role at that time.

You will reach 15 to 20 RM fairly rapidly in some exercises, while in other exercises progress may be slower. This is perfectly normal since some muscles take longer to respond and certain exercises are easier to learn. For some athletes it may take one or two months to reach 15 to 20 RM in all the exercises.

For best results, work out on a regular basis. When on a three-day-per-week program, which is best when first beginning, you must not skip days and say, "I will do four days next week because I only did two this week." This is not effective. Working out more than three days per week does not bring additional benefits and can lead to overtraining and the possibility of injury and soreness. A three-day-per-week program allows for a day's rest in between to give your muscles ample time to fully recover. As a result, it will not interfere with your playing! When you are more fit, working out four to six times per week can be successfully integrated with your playing.

To receive maximum benefit from your training program, you should continue playing in order to constantly make minor adjustments in your execution of the sports skills. Most of the changes will be made subconsciously because of the muscular feel developed when doing the specialized exercises. The changes will feel very natural! However, at this time you should not be going all-out working on technique. Not only may it lead to injury but it does not allow you to concentrate on your form or technique changes.

For example, if you are working on learning or improving running technique, do not run at sprint pace. If you do, you will automatically revert to your former technique. Instead you should embark on slow running, running at a pace that allows you to concentrate on the changes you are making. Once the technique is mastered, gradually increase the speed or intensity of execution until it duplicates what takes place in game play.

Increasing the Difficulty

When you reach 15 to 20 RM for each exercise and the exercises become "easy," you will be ready to move to the next level. At this time the workouts become more strenuous. If you are already strong and have been working out regularly, you can begin on this level, especially if you are already familiar with the exercises. As a result, you can concentrate more on coupling strength with technique. However, when learning a new exercise, start as previously described and gradually build up to the level needed.

Figure 19.5: The arm drive

Whether you use the Active Cords (rubber tubing), dumbbells or barbells, when you regularly reach about 20 RM or more, increase the resistance. Doing this should bring you down to 12 to 15 RM. Then you can work back up to 20 RM and repeat the process. When you do an exercise for 15 to 20 RM it is important that the last repetition be the final one that you can execute with proper technique. Do not, for example, complete 15 or 20 repetitions and still feel refreshed. When you finish the set you should feel slightly out of breath and have muscular fatigue.

Be in tune with your body as you do the exercises. In this way you can you learn which exercises appear to be most effective. You can then make the necessary changes in the exercises or exercise program to produce the desired results. If you need more work on certain muscles or movements, add another set of selected exercises.

Developing Greater Strength

To increase strength after the basic training you should do two to three sets of the key specific exercises. Using greater resistance for greater strength requires warm-up or initial preparation of the muscles. Thus, for the first set (when doing three or more sets), perform 10 repetitions with half the resistance that you will be using in the second set. In the second set, do eight to 10 RM for strength. Follow this with another set of eight to 10 RM if more strength is needed, then complete 15 RM for muscular endurance in the third (or fourth) set.

After you complete the first set, recover for approximately 30 to 60 seconds (longer, if doing explosive strength exercises). Then repeat the same exercise for the second set. You can also do another exercise for different muscles in between sets so that you can complete more exercises in a shorter amount of time.

If you have a very intense program, as is often the case with high-level players, a split program should be considered. This means that you perform the upper- and lower-body exercises twice a week on alternate days with two days of rest for each. In other words, on Mondays and Thursdays you focus upon the upper body; on Tuesdays and Fridays, the lower body; on Wednesdays and Saturdays, spe-

Figure 19.6: Medial/lateral shoulder joint rotation with strength bar

cial workouts to improve other qualities such as flexibility, agility, co-ordination, etc.

Completing three to four sets, a set for warm-up, one to two sets for strength, and a set for endurance is usually sufficient for most players at this time. Do the key special exercises not only to improve your weak actions but also to enhance your strong points. All your exercises should be specific to the sports skills in need of improvement (after your base conditioning).

Do not be misled into believing that you need more and more general strength as practiced by many strength coaches. Additional strength must have a purpose — it must improve specific aspects of your game performance or skill execution. Merely having more strength will not do this for the higher level player. At this time the strength must be coupled with techniques to produce visible results on the field or court. General strength has its greatest effect on youngsters and novices and determines to a good extent how well they play on the field or court.

There is no need for very heavy weights in this program. Keep in mind that if you use too much resistance, your ROM will decrease and your movements will be slow. This, in turn, can negatively affect your playing. So, be sure that you perform the exercises exactly as described regardless of the number of sets and repetitions you do.

You can significantly change how well you play by not only the exercises you use, but also the number of repetitions and sets you complete. For this reason, the structure of your program at this time is critical to your success. The key is to make your workout specific to your sport and position as well as the changes you desire.

Your workout program for strength is different from a program for speed-strength or other qualities. Thus, the workouts must be geared toward the qualities you want to improve as well as the role they play in your particular sport or position.

For example, novices find great improvement in their performance from doing only one set of 15 to 20 RM. The strength gains at this time will raise the level of neuromuscular coordination as well as muscular and cardiovascular endurance which play equally important roles. A more advanced player usually needs greater levels of speed-strength, starting strength and explosive strength. Thus they would do more sets with fewer repetitions (5-10) and more rest inbetween sets. As a result the programs for different levels of players must be distinct, yet can include some of the same exercises.

Cinematogram 19.3: Depth Jump

Frame 1   Frame 2   Frame 3   Frame 4

Frame 5   Frame 6   Frame 7

Speed-Strength and Explosive Training

Strength coupled with speed (speed-strength) and, in many cases, is crucial for almost all athletes and especially for advanced and elite players. Speed-strength and explosive training are the keys to increasing speed and quickness. However, such training should be done only after you have a well-established strength base.

The introduction of speed-strength work should be slow and gradual. It should begin with relatively easy preparatory exercises as well as exercises with strength and explosive movements. One example is to hold a squat position with resistance for up to four to five seconds and then explode or jump upward. To ensure that you introduce the explosive work slowly and gradually, begin with activities such as simple skipping, hopping, jumping, leaping and bounding. These activities prepare the muscles for more intense work later.

If you strength train three times a week, introductory speed-strength work is done on the alternate days but no more than twice a week. If you are on a four-day split program, speed-strength work can be sequenced with the strength training. In this case, the speed-strength work is done first (after a vigorous warm-up) and the workout is concluded with strength and in some cases endurance work. Depending upon your level of fitness and mastery of the exercises, increase the intensity after four to eight weeks or more. When you are capable of correctly doing high-intensity jumps you will be ready for a maximum-intensity workout. At this time you should gradually increase the number of explosive exercises and/or the number of sets done for each exercise. But do not do more than 10 repetitions of each explosive exercise.

Beginners and players aged 6-12 should use speed-strength and explosive training sparingly. Initially, aerobic capabilities and strength are most important, and up to 80 percent of your training should be devoted to this. Speed work should comprise about 20 percent of your workouts. As you get older and more proficient, do three to four speed-strength or lead-up plyometric exercises for one to two sets in the training session before the strength or endurance training. The work intensity for advanced players (late teens and older) is very high. Be-

Cinematogram 19.4: Bounding

Frame 1   *Frame 2*   *Frame 3*   *Frame 4*

cause of this, more rest is needed between sets (three to eight minutes), making the workouts longer, up to two hours, if they include special strength training.

Speed-strength and explosive training, especially shock training, should be done only in the specialized period of training. Because this type of training has a strong residual effect, you should stop at least one to two weeks before competition. This is important to give the muscles ample time to fully adapt and be ready for peak performance.

Speed Training

Speed and quickness training (sprints, explosive strength exercises and explosive agility/cutting exercises) should be done no more than two times a week, except when learning technique. When sprinting, it is important to maintain good running technique. When fatigue sets in, your technique changes and you will develop different neuro-muscular pathways. When the nervous system is fresh you can duplicate the correct technique to ensure the fastest running and cutting. This is why speed and quickness should always precede other types of training.

Do not embark on all-out speed training when you are also doing heavy strength training. The two are not compatible. Intense strength training should be decreasing and speed-strength training increasing as you introduce all-out speed and quickness training. Explosive exercises are best suited to preparing the muscles for fast actions.

If you are in the process of modifying your running or cutting technique, you should not do all-out speed training because you will automatically return to your old form. Once you master the necessary technique you can then gradually increase speed and quickness while still maintaining good technique.

Overspeed training (running faster than you can) can be done at the same time as speed work. When executing overspeed training, you teach the nervous and muscular systems to experience faster and quicker movements. There are various ways to achieve overspeed, and the application of each method must be quite precise. For example, in downhill running, the distance must not be very long and the angle of the slope no greater than three to five degrees. Running with a parachute and then releasing, or jumping and running with extra weight can be effective; but how much weight and where it is distributed are the keys to the success of the training. Because overspeed methods require considerable detail and precision and can be easily misinterpreted, they are not discussed here.

Integrated Training

Most often, you develop separate training programs for qualities such as strength, flexibility, neuromuscular coordination (technique), speed-strength (power), muscular strength and cardiovascular endurance. How to integrate these different workouts into one or more training sessions thus becomes very important, especially in view of the limited time you may have. The following is the general order in

Figure 19.7: Lying front arm raises

which you should train the different physical qualities within one session.

1. Technique (Skill) Learning

To learn or modify technique most effectively, your nervous system must be in a high energy state. You must be alert to and aware of exactly what you are doing. You must be tuned into the feedback you receive and be capable of making the changes needed to improve your skill. Because of this, technique must be first in your training. Note that this is predicated on the fact that you already have base levels of strength and endurance.

2. Speed and Explosive Training

If no technique work is done, speed and explosive training move to the number one position. Be sure to have a good warm-up to prepare the muscles for speed or explosive power exercises. If you wish to do both technique and speed work in the same session, the amount of technique work should be minimal and used mainly for reinforcement of particular coordinations or as a warm-up to the speed and explosive training.

3. Specialized Strength Work

All specialized strength exercises that duplicate particular aspects of your sports skills must be done prior to other types of strength training. At this time you must be relatively fresh and energetic so that you can concentrate on repeating the exact movements to develop a

Figure 19.8: Reverse sit-up

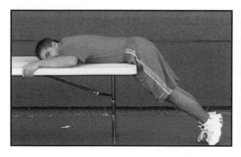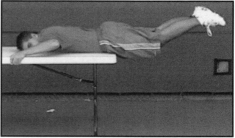

Figure 19.9: Reverse back raise

muscular feel for them. Thus, specialized exercises follow speed and explosive work, but only if you are not fatigued.

4. General All-Around Strength Training

Training that is general, such as all-around conditioning, and is not specific to the joint actions involved in specific skills can be done when in a fatigued state. Because of this, it follows the other types of training that require high levels of energy. General training is often done after practice.

5. Muscular Endurance/Cardiovascular Endurance

Usually these two qualities are combined but they can also be done separately. For example, there are instances when you must work on muscular endurance that is needed in a typical game. Such workouts are localized to particular joint actions, as for example doing 30-50 repetitioins of the knee drive to develop the hip flexors to maintain strike length in you running. Cardiovascular work may automatically be included if it involves large body parts.

In cardiovascular work, the total body is usually involved, such as in long-distance or cross-country running, cycling or rowing. Endurance should always be the last type of training done in the session. Aerobic training should never be used as a warm-up. Light jogging during which the heart rate stays well below the training zone is acceptable for warm-up and recovery. To have a training effect in endurance work, you must have the heart rate in a higher range.

Elite athletes usually combine two or more types of training. Most common is undertaking technique work with speed or explosive actions. High-level athletes are capable of doing this because of their highly developed skill and ability. Moreover, the work on technique usually involves only minor adjustments.

In-Season Maintenance

Increases in strength and other physical qualities are not called for during the competitive season. Maintaining and perfecting your skill, and developing strategy based on your physical and technical abilities becomes most important at this time. However, you can continue to practice speed and quickness work in sports that rely on these qualities. In addition, explosive cutting and running and other forms of speed-strength work may be done. The speed and explosive training should maintain the achieved strength levels. If not, maintenance work should be incorporated.

If your levels of strength and endurance begin to decrease, you should continue to train one to two days per week with one set of the key exercises. Two sets may be necessary in certain exercises. The exact number of repetitions and sets will depend on your level of fitness and your in-season goals. For most players, one set for 10 to 20 RM is sufficient when done twice a week. Advanced players may require more work to maintain speed and quickness if the speed and explosive actions performed during competition are insufficient to maintain achieved strength levels.

If you stop your training and devote your time solely to competitions, you may experience a decrease in your strength and other qualities, and find your skill execution changing. This is especially true as

Figure 19.10: Single leg jumps

you age. But by maintaining your strength and flexibility levels, you can maintain the ability to play basically the same way in the later years as in your youth. Increase your physical abilities and you will play on a higher skill level.

Do not copy what many professional players practice. For example, most major league baseball pitchers (and other position players) report to camp in an out-of-shape state without having done any serious throwing or conditioning for many months. They begin camp with easy throwing to regain their mechanics and to get accustomed to the throwing. Because they do not want to experience injury, teams limit their throwing and it is usually not until the second month of the in-season that they regain form and can pitch a whole game. As a result, they are usually lucky to throw as they did in the previous year. In only very rare cases do you see improvement over the previous season.

Principles of Training

How you work out is critical to your development. To get the best results, you should adhere to the following principles of training:

Individualization

You are a unique individual and will respond to exercises differently from another athlete. Aside from the obvious structural differences there are also physiological differences in your muscular, circulatory and nervous systems that require individualization in your

Figure 19.11: Leg extension

program. This is why you must be the one to decide the types of exercises needed, the number of sets and reps, and the method of training. Your training program should be for you and only you.

You should never imitate someone else's program. Because someone you know may have responded quickly to a program does not mean that your body will also respond in the same manner. Each of you has his/her own rate of development and level of potential.

If you copy someone else's program regardless of how successful it is, you take a chance of getting injured. Not only may the resistance be greater than what your muscles and joints can handle, but the way the exercise is executed by another person may not fit the way your body is designed to move. In these instances there is a high likelihood of injury. Your program must be individualized, just as your playing ability is very individual. You must develop your physical abilities in tandem with your skill (technique) execution.

Gradualness

Regardless of your exercise program or level of performance, any increase in speed, flexibility, strength, resistance, repetitions or sets should be very gradual. For example, if you are accustomed to doing 15 RM for two sets, you should not suddenly increase to 25 to 50 repetitions or do four to five sets. Your body is not ready for such abrupt changes, and injuries may occur. Thus, you should incorporate all changes gradually.

Progressiveness

In order to show continual increases in speed or muscular strength or endurance, you must gradually but progressively increase the amount of resistance (intensity), the number of exercises, the total number of repetitions (volume), or the rate of work. If you continue to work at the same level and do the same number of exercises, sets and reps, etc., you will only maintain your achieved levels.

Overload

Overload is related to progressiveness. It means that you undertake more than what your body is accustomed to. For example, in order to develop greater strength you must use additional resistance. To increase flexibility you must increase the range of motion. Other ways to achieve overload include increasing the rate of work: doing the exercises at a slightly faster rate of speed or in an explosive manner. These latter methods, however, apply more to advanced players and should be used only after you have achieved base levels of strength and endurance.

Awareness

Awareness means being cognizant of what is happening to your body. You should learn what each exercise feels like and how your body responds to it. In time, you develop a muscle memory so that when you execute the exercise (or skill) you can tell immediately if it is working for you or if something is amiss. When things do not feel right, you should check to see if your execution is correct or if there is some other problem that is interfering.

To help you be aware, you should keep a record of your workouts. Record not only the resistance, sets and repetitions for each exercise, but also how you feel. Make notations of what you experience, both mentally and physically.

This is especially important for women who respond differently in each phase of the menstrual cycle. Some women do their best work (or playing) after menstruation, while others perform better at the actual time of menstruation. For this reason, you should determine when you can do your most productive work and schedule the workouts around the menstrual cycle. In general, stay away from very strenuous activity (such as using heavy resistance) during the menstrual period.

Consistency

Without consistency in your exercise program, all the work that you do may come to naught. For example, after each workout your energy supply is exhausted. It is replaced while you are resting and sleeping when additional energy supplies for later use are deposited (supercompensation). If you do not exercise sufficiently to use this extra energy that has been deposited, the body will reabsorb it and you may be left with the same energy as before. For example, I am sure you have noticed that when you have not played or worked out for a while you actually become more tired than if you were active throughout the entire day.

Consistency, which means doing the exercises or training on a regular basis, is the key to success. You should set aside the time needed in your busy schedule so that the exercise program and practice become as important as your other activities. If for some reason you are unable to work out for a week or two, start your exercises again upon your return using less resistance. In one or two days you should get back into the groove of doing the exercises and seeing results.

Conclusion

Many players want a daily prescription for what they should do for every workout. But as discussed here, this is impossible because each workout must be based on your unique abilities. This is also why the exact number of sets, repetitions and weights that you should use in the different periods of training are not presented. Use the general guidelines on how the workouts should progress from the beginning of the year up to the time of competition. You have a great arsenal of exercises from which to choose and different types of training programs to bring about increases in strength, speed-strength, endurance, explosiveness, etc. It is simply a matter of selecting the exercises that will best enhance your abilities and incorporating them within the guidelines presented. For help in specific sports, see some of the books recommended in previous chapters.

Coaches have a tendency to have all players execute the same workouts mainly for efficiency and convenience. But to maximize each player's program requires individualized work which takes more time and effort. Thus, the burden should not rest solely on the shoulders of the coach; it must also be your responsibility. Only you can do the work, and if you are serious about your playing and want to improve to your potential, then it behooves you to take a very strong interest in determining your abilities and the best methods for improvement. You cannot rely only on the head coach or even the strength coaches.

Establishing your own individualized training program is not difficult. If you have come this far in the book you should already have a good understanding of what is involved in improving your performance. Guidelines on how you should construct your program, which exercises you should include and how many sets and reps should be done, have been presented. This should give you enough information to guide your training program. If you keep a diary you will know exactly what you are doing and will be able to make adjustments as you progress. Do not rely on others to program the training for you. You must be actively involved in the process to succeed.

Unfortunately, many training programs do not follow well-proven guidelines, mainly because the players do not train or stay in shape on a year-round basis. Because of this, general conditioning and preparation for play often occur in the preseason, and the early games of the season are often used to continue preparing you for more intense playing. Some programs even include heavy weight training at the beginning of the in-season. This should not be done unless you are very weak or out of shape, as it interferes greatly with your skills. All such work should be done well in advance of your playing.

By adhering to the recommendations presented in this book you will not only be able to play your best but also improve your playing every year. You will be able to play at your best for the entire game.

For More Information

After reading and possibly rereading portions of the book, you probably have questions. To help answer them I recommend that you see archives of past newsletters that appear on **www.DrYessis.com**. In every issue there are one or two topics that deal with training as well as different aspects of selected sports.

In addition, you may wish to send any questions you have pertaining to the various aspects discussed in this book. If there is a sufficient number of such questions, an answer will appear from Dr. Yessis on the website. If there is sufficient interest, an interactive site will be developed so that you can write in your questions and have other people respond along with Dr. Yessis. In this way, we can open discussion on various topics and, hopefully, come to some worthwhile conclusions that can be put into practice to make your training and/ or coaching more productive.

In addition, you may be interested in some of the other services available from Sports Training, Inc. Please refer to the Yessis System of Improving Performance at **www.DrYessis.com** for more information about the equipment and books mentioned in this text. You can also contact Dr. Yessis at P.O. Box 460429, Escondido, CA, 92046 or telephone 760-480-0558.

NOTES:

Chapter 20
Tips to Maintain Your Program

Many athletes are successful in initiating an exercise program but tend to maintain it for only short periods of time. Because of this, they rarely see all of the positive results that are possible. To prevent this from happening to you, and to help you maintain your program, the following are some time-proven tips that have worked successfully for many athletes:

1. *Schedule Exercise or Training First.* Exercise and/or training should come first. This may seem heretical as it appears to take away from your job, school work and other chores which are extremely important. However, setting aside a time to exercise is a key element in continuing a program.

   For example, by maintaining your exercise program, your mental work will improve. This, in turn, makes you more efficient and productive, which then allows you to get more accomplished. This saves you time, makes you feel better and allows you to improve and play better. Squeezing in exercise and training only when you have time will lead to certain defeat.

2. *The Exercise/Training Lifestyle.* Exercise and training should be a part of your lifestyle. In essence, you must develop the habit of participation on a regular basis. Once the habit is established

it is difficult to break. But in order to establish the habit, it must become a part of your normal, everyday routine.

3. *Give a Particular Workout a Fair Chance*. First exposure to any new exercise or training program can be uncomfortable. This also holds true for many other areas of life. But by persevering in the activity, having effective instruction in the basic techniques and understanding the role of such training can lead to enjoyment and pleasure. Very few activities are truly enjoyed from the first day of participation; you can learn to enjoy the workout!

4. *Start Slowly*. Your body needs time to adapt in order for the gains to be seen and, most importantly, for the gains to last. Progress in the program can be fast, but any increases in volume, intensity, exercises, etc., should be slow and gradual.

5. *Keep It Individualized*. The training program must be individualized to fit you. This means that you should make progress at your own rate and the training program must be based on your capabilities—not on someone else's.

6. *Just Do It*. Some athletes are great at creating excuses for why they cannot work out. They procrastinate and say they will make it up or do more at a later time. This is acceptable at times, but chronic procrastination can defeat all the good intentions.

   One or two skipped workouts can be made up quickly. But if you start skipping more sessions, it becomes important to determine the reason and the remedial steps that can be taken immediately. Not only does procrastinating jeopardize the success of any program, it is also stressful and lowers your self-esteem, further snuffing your motivation to stick with the program.

7. *Keep a Workout Diary*. When you keep a diary of the workouts, either by yourself or in conjunction with others, it can be used to evaluate your progress. The diary should show whether

progress is commensurate with your abilities and level of fitness or whether any problems are developing along the way.

8. *Forget About Being Ultra-Perfect.* Many athletes look for perfection. Even youngsters hesitate to undertake an activity if they do not feel they can do it well. The key here is to participate and not always be concerned with the outcome in the initial stages. Participate to reap the enjoyment from the activity, and achieve a certain level of playing ability or skill mastery. Let perfection become important as you approach high or elite levels.

9. *Half a Workout is Better Than None.* If it is impossible to have a full workout, doing a partial one is still of great benefit. Flexibility here is important mentally as it is physically.

10. *Give It 6-8 Weeks.* Six to eight weeks is the minimum amount of time it takes to develop a new habit. It is also the length of time it takes to experience physiological changes in the body as a result of the exercise/training program. These are the long-lasting benefits that usually hook you on the activity and incline you toward greater or more intense participation.

11. *Do Not Obsess Over Food.* Proper nutrition is critical for your best performances. However, being obsessive about the types and amounts of foods you eat is detrimental to producing the best results. The key is to avoid thinking in terms of good foods or bad foods. Instead, think variety and whole, real food. All natural foods have value. The main items to beware of are the saturated fats, trans-fatty acids and processed foods.

12. *Set Realistic Goals.* When goals are realistic they can be attained. You can then achieve the success and satisfaction that will drive you on.

13. *Give It Your Best Shot.* Working out requires hard work, not only to learn well but also to improve your abilities. When you realize that it takes hard work to achieve the gains you desire, you will be more inclined to do the work. As a result, you will

also experience greater satisfaction and enjoyment. Remind yourself of the benefits.

14. *Get Started*. Once you start in an effective manner, you will be more inclined to continue. Very often the most difficult part of an exercise or training program is taking the first step. Once you take it, however, you overcome much of your anxiety so that you can really get "into" the activity.

15. *Draw Up an Agreement*. Have an agreement with a coach, family member or friend. Putting it in writing is a very important step for some individuals. With a specific contract, the actual days on which your workouts will take place and exactly what you will be doing is spelled out. The agreement should be long-term and can include specific rewards and punishments.

16. *Say, "Yes, I Can."* Research shows that affirmations, simple positive statements that reflect your beliefs and intents, are powerful ways to keep on track or to change for the better. When you think positively, you will get positive results. The goal is to focus on the process of making positive changes and on improvements, not on perfection. The great thing about specific training is that it is not an end in itself. It is a means of achieving other goals.

17. *Keep an Eye on the Future*. Focus more closely on where your technical and playing level will be in the next few months or even years. If you keep your goals in mind, especially long-term goals, you will be more likely to succeed and not be set back by any minor failures. This is a great way to maintain a positive, long-range outlook.

18. *Visualize Success*. When you see yourself performing well in your imagination, it helps to increase self-confidence. If you can see it and believe it, it can be realized.

NOTES:

Index

sprint technique, **41**–43; and stretching, 147; training program for, 17, 191; and weight training, 13; when to start, 2. *see also* teenagers

cholesterol, 166

circling, 44

coaches, 1, 6, 9–10, 32, 33, 34, 188, 215

competition: emphasis on, 1–2; as phase of development, 17, 18; training during, 190, 195–96, 211–12

concentration and nutrition, 181–82

concentric strength, 95–96, 97, 138

contracts, 222

cooling off, 170–71. *see also* recovery; rest

coordination, 137–38, 158, 161. *see also* agility

core training, 151

cross-country skiing, 127–28

cutting: exercises for, 143, 193–94; side, **135–37**; in team sports, 133–34, 139; technique, 35, 137–38, 139–42, 144

cycling exercise routine, 197–98

D

depth jump, 115, **205**

depth perception, 160, 161

diaries, workout, 214, 216, 220–21

diet. *see* eating habits; nutrition

discus, **67,** 71

distance running, **31,** 37, **39, 42,** 45, 47

diving, 49

downhill running, 208

drills, 1–2, 142–43

drugs, performance enhancing, 183–84, 185–88

E

East Europeans, 2, 115, 126, 184–85

eating habits: drinking water, 170–74; and early development, 14; not obsessing over, 221; and nutrition, 163–70; and supplements, 174–75; timing of meals, 179–81. *see also* nutrition

eccentric strength, 95–96, 97, 117, 138

EMB (eye-mind-body speed), 157–58, 161

emotional needs and nutrition, 181–82

endurance, 121–31; and aerobic energy sources, 123–26, 176; and aerobic training for, 126–31; and drugs, 183, 187; in integrated training, 210; and muscle fibers, 4, 210–11; psychological, 122–23; and speed events, 121–22; and strength training, 98, 104

energy: and aerobic conditioning, 123–26; how it's produced, 175–79

energy bars, 170

equilibrium. *see* balance

exercises. *see* plyometric exercises; speed training; strength training; *and specific sports and parts of the body*

Explosive Running (Yessis), 47

explosive training/explosivity. *see* speed; speed training

eye-mind-body speed (EMB), 157–58, 161

F

falling, technique of, 155–56

fats: effect of, in your body, 175–77, 178–79; in your diet, 164–65, 167, 169, 170, 180

feinting actions, 141

figure skating, 11

finger flexion, **80, 81**

flexibility (range of motion), 145–50; and agility, 138, 143; bad stretching for, 146, 147–48; good stretching for, 146–47, 148–50; kinds of stretching for, 145–46; and specialized exercises, 100

food. *see* eating habits; nutrition

football, **62,** 116–17, 128, 133–34

forward head, 23

functional strength, 97–98

G

Gatorade, 171

genetics, 2–4

glute-ham-gastroc raise, **46, 107**–8
goal setting, 221
golf, 28–29, 66, 76, 78, **79,** 100
grip exercise, **110**
gymnastics, 11, 139, 152

H

hand exercises, **80, 81,** 110
handball, **74,** 76, 78, **78,** 80
hang time, 54
Harrison, Bill, 162
health, 22, 183, 186. *see also* injuries
heart rate, 129, 130–31
heel raise, 46, 56, **56, 190**
height improvement, 25–26
high jumping, 29
hip joint exercises, 22–23, **71,** 90, 107–8, 143, 149
hitting, 73–81; exercises, 80, 81, 146, 154; grip, 80; technique, 73–80; and weight shift, 73–74
hydration, 170–74

I

in-season training, 211–12. *see also* competition
injuries: from balance exercises, 156; jumping, 55; kicking, 89; and nutrition, 180; from posture problems, 23, 24; preventing, 92–93, 101, 114, 134; rehabilitation of, 191; running, 40; strength training, 105, 106, 201, 213, 214; stretching, 91, 145–46, 147; throwing, 69, 70
instructors. *see* coaches
integrated training, 208–11
internet-based training programs, 161
isometric strength, 95–96

J

Jordan, Michael, 31
jumping, 49–57; exercises, 56–57, 153, **191, 192, 205, 207, 211**; as speed training, 49, **115**–16, 117; technique, 29, 50–55; universality of, 30

K

kicking, 83–90; exercises, 90, 146; injuries, 89; technique, 83–89; universality of, 30, 83
kinesthetic sense, 153
knee joint exercises, **90,** 107, 149, **198, 199**

L

lactic acid levels, 125–26
ladder drills, 142
leg exercises, **90, 192, 211, 212**
long jumping, 55
lower-body exercises: for all-around strength, 191–92; in base training, 106–7; for endurance, 127–28; for flexibility, 149
lunges, 150, 154, **193**

M

machine weights, 102
medial/lateral shoulder joint rotation, **204**
medial rotation, **72, 204**
medicine balls, **72,** 102, **102**
mental skills: and nutrition, 178, 181–82; and rest, 196; and strength training, 93–94; used in learning sports skills, 32, 33. *see also* psychological attributes
midsection exercises, 26, 90, 106, 192
motor skills, 32–34, 92
muscle fibers, 3–4, 127, 128, 210–11. *see also* neuromuscular system
muscle resiliency, exercises for, 46–47

N

neck exercises, 23
neuromuscular system: and cycling, 197–98, 198–99; early development of, 12; response to learning skills, 32–34, 99; and speed training, 119
novices: and annual training program, 191; and gaining general strength, 204, 205; speed